A Way Out
Of
No Way

To Bruce, + Jeannette,

Keep Faith,

Andrew

A
Way
Out Of
No
Way

The Spiritual Memoirs of

ANDREW YOUNG

THOMAS NELSON PUBLISHERS
Nashville • Atlanta • London • Vancouver

Published in Nashville, Tennessee, by Thomas Nelson, Inc., Publishers, and distributed in Canada by Word Communications, Ltd., Richmond, British Columbia, and in the United Kingdom by Word (UK), Ltd., Milton Keynes, England.

This book was originally published in hardcover by Thomas Nelson, Inc.

Unless otherwise noted, Scripture quotations are from the NEW KING JAMES VERSION of the Bible. Copyright © 1979, 1980, 1982, Thomas Nelson, Inc., Publishers.

Scripture quotations noted KJV are from The Holy Bible, KING JAMES VERSION.

Scripture quotations noted RSV are from the REVISED STANDARD VERSION of the Bible. Copyright © 1946, 1952, 1971, 1973 by the Division of Christian Education of the National Council of the Churches of Christ in the U.S.A. Used by permission.

Scripture quotations noted NIV are taken from the HOLY BIBLE, NEW INTERNATIONAL VERSION®. Copyright © 1973, 1978, 1984 by International Bible Society. Used by permission of Zondervan Bible Publishing House. All rights reserved.

The "NIV" and "New International Version" trademarks are registered in the United States Patent and Trademark Office by International Bible Society. Use of either trademark requires the permission of International Bible Society.

Scripture quotations noted TEV are from the *Good News Bible,* Old Testament © 1976 by the American Bible Society; New Testament © 1966, 1971, 1976 American Bible Society. Used by permission.

Library of Congress Cataloging-in-Publication Data
Young, Andrew, 1932–
    A way out of no way / Andrew Young.
      P.   cm.
   ISBN 0-8407-6998-9 (hc)
   ISBN 0-7852-7508-8 (pb)
    1. Young, Andrew, 1932–   . 2. Legislators—United States—Biography. 3. Ambassadors—United States—Biography. 4. United States. Congress. House—Biography. 5. United Church of Christ—United States—Clergy—Biography. 6. Civil rights workers—United States—Biography. 7. Afro-Americans—Biography. 8. Afro-Americans—Civil rights. 9. Civil rights movements—United States—History—20th century.   I. Title.
E840.8.Y64A3   1994
973.92′092—dc20
[B]   93-35738
                                                           CIP

Printed in the United States of America
4 5 6 7 8 9 - 01 00 99 98 97 96

□

To those who seek the Way amid the questions,
conflict, and confusion of our time.

Contents

☐

Acknowledgments   ix

August 1993   xi

Introduction   1

1. A Time for Decision   7

2. On Kings Mountain   15

3. Answering the Call   25

4. Not My Will   34

5. Changing the World   47

6. Breaking Down Walls   61

7. Building Leaders   73

8. Bless Those That Persecute You   86

9. The Spirit Is A'movin' All Over the Land   99

10. Lead Kindly Light   114

11. Blessed Are the Peacemakers   127

12. When All God's Chillun Get Together   140

13. A Way Out of No Way   151

Notes   171

Acknowledgments

The publication of this memoir began with a chance meeting in the Atlanta airport with Sam Moore, Chairman and CEO of Thomas Nelson Publishers. I'll always be grateful to Sam for suggesting that his readers would be interested in the spiritual and motivational aspects of my life and work—what's behind the public man.

Lawrence Jordan and Tom Dent started me remembering and recording the exciting years of my youth, and Janet Hulstrand, Paul Smith, and Tony Stanley helped clarify the pages that seemed to rush from my little computer whenever I could slow down and calm my spirit to reflect on the miracle of life, especially my life.

Thanks also to Maggie Womack, Doug Gatlin, and Kay Jackson for organizing my schedule to make room for writing, and to R. K. Sehgal and the Law Companies Group for being sensitive to the spiritual foundations of even the engineering and environmental business.

The support, encouragement, and professional guidance of Lonnie Hull DuPont and Sheryl Taylor led me from paper to print with the Thomas Nelson team, making the process a true joy and excitement.

But the story truly comes from my parents, family, and friends who loved me into an understanding of God's love. My wife, Jean, especially reminded me of many of the things I wanted to forget and the fact that our love grew stronger with each challenge. Andrea, Lisa, Paula, and Bo, my children, read and contributed comments to the process, as did my sons-in-law Tony, Douglas, and Hilary.

In the depths of my heart, however, it is the love for my grandchildren that motivates me to give a spiritual legacy to Taylor Marie, Kemet, Lena, and all that are yet to come. Hopefully they will understand that to God be the glory for the things we have done.

August 1993

It was hot. It's always hot in Washington, D.C. during the month of August. The crowd gathered from all over the country. We were celebrating the thirtieth anniversary of the 1963 March on Washington where Martin Luther King, Jr. electrified the nation with his eloquent cry for freedom and justice in the now famous "I Have a Dream" speech.

I had first marched in Washington as a young minister, driving up from Georgia in 1957 for the Prayer Pilgrimage which simply pleaded to the nation to give us the ballot. We returned in 1963 to seek a desegregated America where, in Martin's words, "A man might be judged by the content of his character, rather than the color of his skin."

Then again in 1968 in the Poor People's Campaign the nation's poor—black, brown, red, and white—joined in a quest for economic justice in America. No nation as rich as ours should have so many people isolated on islands of poverty in such a sea of material wealth.

Washington, D.C. is not only our nation's capital, it is the place to which we come to bring ideas and build a majority consensus in this government "of the people, by the people and for the people." It is also a place of remembrance and celebration in the struggle to achieve democracy and prosperity among the peoples who have gathered here from all over the world—people who daily strive to become a family, truly "one nation, under God, indivisible."

I was asked by the press whether we would be coming back to Washington to celebrate the fortieth anniversary in 2003, or did I think we could solve our problems by then? I replied that like the Jews have celebrated the Passover as their time of understanding of God's deliverance, I expected those Americans whose ancestors were brought to these shores as slaves, artisans, and indentured servants would continue coming back to Washington to celebrate survival and deliverance.

Sitting on the steps of the Lincoln Memorial and watching people come from all over the world, I realized that I had been a part of one of our nation's most powerful and productive periods of history. I had marched here with Martin Luther King, Jr., I had served as a member of the United States Congress and I had represented the United States as ambassador to the United Nations. As mayor of Atlanta, I came to Washington on many occasions on behalf of the cities. And now I was back again, this time as a private citizen, as vice-chairman of Law Companies Group, a worldwide engineering and environmental consulting firm with offices in forty countries on five continents, and as co-chairman of the Atlanta Committee to Organize the Olympic Games in 1996.

Washington, D.C. is like a second home for me and for much of the world. And on this hot August day as flags waved from Ethiopia, Liberia, Nigeria, Haiti, and even Korea, it was clear that the deliverance which we celebrated was the dream of the entire world. As we heard songs from Israel and prayers from Christians, Moslems, Hindus, and Greek Orthodox, it was clear to me that the press which primarily focused on the numbers of people and the organizational problems did not catch the significance of this celebration of the progress of humanity toward becoming human family.

By God's amazing grace, I have been a part of this movement in history. And not even in my wildest dreams could I have anticipated such a future—especially when I was a student in Washington many years ago . . .

Introduction

☐

In 1951 as a confused and bewildered nineteen-year-old approaching graduation from Howard University, I could not have predicted that my life nor the times in which I've lived would change in such meaningful ways. The forty years since that time have brought about such positive fulfillment in matters of human rights and relationships. I don't believe that these changes are accidental, the spontaneous generation of order out of chaos.

These changes all evolved through the actions of people —people of faith who courageously responded to the conflict, chaos, violence, and hatred around them with a mysterious but magnificent faith. These people believed that there is purpose in human existence and that the Creator of life and time, spirit and matter, somehow is present with his creatures and continues to be involved with ordinary men and women. These very people, in critical moments in their lives and history, received special insight and the courage and the will to act. Because of them the world has changed. When seen in this context, life suddenly makes sense; good things happen in the least likely situations, and a certain divine destiny seems fulfilled.

This is a book about life—life as I have observed it, lived it, and most importantly, come to understand it.

I can only explain my own life and the events of the times in which I've lived in the context of faith—a biblical faith that continues to see the hand of God working in the affairs of the children of creation. I bring no argument here, no attempt to convince or convert. This is a simple proclamation of my understanding of life. My life has unfolded around me in ways that fill me with awe and wonder.

I am not alone or special in this experience. Most of the successful men and women I have known can point to moments of destiny in their lives—times when a simple decision produced complex and meaningful results which were totally beyond anticipation. It is the interrelationship of the multiple coincidences of one's life that makes many of us believe that there is divine purpose and power in human life. Undergirding all that we can touch, see, hear, and smell is a spiritual reality to which we must learn to be sensitive.

My life only makes any sense when I include the spiritual dimension. The events that produce genuine change or meaningful success always involve a dimension that is beyond the obvious political, social, or personal forces. Something *extra* pulls all these energies and insights together creating something greater than the sum of its parts.

Before America was ribboned with expressways and interstate highways, it was necessary to follow small and rather insignificant highway signs through the bustling and busy streets of America. These signs could guide you through the most confusing towns. But if you didn't learn to look for the signs, it was easy to get lost. After driving for a mile or two with no visible sign to guide you, it was advisable to stop and ask directions, or retrace your route to discover where you missed a turn or strayed from the designated highway. It was absolutely imperative to follow the signs to your destination or you could wander dozens of miles in the wrong direction.

Hopefully this book will offer a few clues on how to follow the Spirit and read the signs of the times in your life. The signs we need are always present, but too often we think we already know where we are going and reject the designated route. God gives us that freedom too. Thankfully there is a clearly marked route for each of us. We must only choose to follow it.

Thomas Kelly, a Pennsylvania Quaker, wrote in *Testament of Devotion*:

> Deep within us all there is an amazing inner sanctuary of the soul, a holy place, a Divine Center, a speaking Voice, to which we may continuously return. Eternity is at our hearts pressing upon our time-worn lives, warming us with intimations of an astounding destiny, calling us home unto Itself.[1]

The testimony of men and women down through the ages can help us to discover or discern a spiritual direction for our lives. Saint Augustine, the African theologian of the early church, struggled and strained to make his own way for thirty-five years, yet he only found peace and purpose in his life when he admitted prayerfully, "For you have made us for yourself and our hearts are restless, till we find their rest in you."[2]

Throughout the centuries many men and women have experienced similar Augustinian awakenings. Diverse events that seem unrelated take on meaning and purpose far beyond anything originally discernable upon reflection.

In this book I would like to share with you some of my own stories of faith—situations in which I have seemingly been accidentally caught up in God's plan. I always went along willingly, because through the years I have learned that "God moves in mysterious ways, his wonders to perform." I have begun continually to look for the hand of God in my daily life. I have come to believe that God truly *is* with us. God is with me and with you. God is with our children and with our parents. God is with our business partners and with our competitors. God is with our friends and with our enemies. In retrospect, events that seem accidental or even tragic at the time of occurrence turn out to be more developments in God's continuously unfolding and marvelously meaningful plan.

This *is* our Father's world, and we must lend listening ears to the songs and signs of life found in nature, the events of history, and the social encounters of our daily routine. We never know when or how new meaning might break through. We can't predict when a new understanding might emerge or a divine insight might be revealed to illuminate our dark and lonely paths. We don't know how God might act to open up a new way, a new joy, a new freedom, and a new, more glorious life.

For me, life really did begin at forty. I was sworn in as a member of the Ninety-third Congress of the United States a few weeks before my fortieth birthday. Five years later, I was United States ambassador to the United Nations, then mayor of Atlanta for eight years. I was surprisingly successful in each of these potentially difficult situations. Life seemed to know no limits for me, and few problems took more than a few days to work out some approach toward a solution. But then, like a hurricane ending a wonderful summer at the beach, things changed dramatically.

During the past two years, many clouds have darkened my life. First, I lost the Democratic primary for governor of Georgia. That was a major setback, but I have never been so totally dominated by politics that I could not readily adjust to alternatives. Second, after being blessed with thirty-seven years of marriage, four wonderful children, and three fabulous grandchildren, I learned that my wife, Jean, had developed cancer. Finally, the very week that she came home from surgery, my son, during his first week in college, was stopped by police one block from the campus and brutally beaten for no apparent reason, within full view of witnesses. It has been indeed a dark time in my life—a life that, heretofore, seemed charmed and protected from personal tragedy and adversity.

Yet even amidst these dark times, the presence of God has been all too clear. Even in tragedy and calamity there is newfound strength and meaning. The way I must now follow is not yet clear to me, but as I remain sensitive to the hand and plan of God amid the turmoil and confusion, I see that I have not been abandoned by the Lord of life and creation. Just as God has led me in the past so will God lead me now and in the future. As the old hymn goes, "Through many dangers, toils and snares I have already come. 'Tis grace hath brought me safe thus far, and grace will lead me home."

The darkness of trying times can filter out the glare and make clearer the presence of God. The attention is concentrated in the darkness. Nothing can be taken for granted. The soft light of the Spirit can serve as a clear beacon toward the future. Perhaps this is why so many people find faith in tough times.

But one does not need tragedy to learn of the presence of God and the work of the Spirit. We can also learn from the cloud of witnesses—previous generations that have gone before. The experiences of others in the Scriptures, the church, and the day-to-day life that we share also can be trainers of the Spirit.

None of the peace and purpose that I now enjoy was apparent to me during the early years of my life. The racially segregated South placed chains on my mind in spite of the prayers and teaching of loving parents. I could not even conceive of the success I have enjoyed, much less dream or aspire to the heights to which my career has soared. There was no way that I could have imagined participating in the decisions and actions which have helped to shape the world in this century. But an old saying out of the jargon of slavery affirms, "The Lord can make a way out of no way."

For me, only the power of God could have taken the weak and undisciplined creature that I am and made me a part of the team of diverse characters that surrounded Martin Luther King, Jr. and transformed the South. Time and again, when we did our best and tried everything we could think of, we saw only failure, frustration, and no way out. Somehow, each time the Lord made a way.

Despite the setbacks my family has personally suffered through in the past year, God has smiled on me. And I can show you some of my journey.

1

A Time
for
Decision

My father's new Oldsmobile purred reassuringly, providing a cocoon of security that carried us through the silent southern night. In 1951 there was no hotel where a black family could spend the night between Washington, D.C. and our destination in North Carolina. We had to drive straight through.

I didn't mind driving through the night. While my parents and my brother, Walter, slept, I had solitude to think. The quiet was especially precious to me now. In the silence and darkness, gripping the wheel and watching the headlights cut a swath of light across the blacktop, I could wrestle with my most pressing problem. How was I going to tell my father that I didn't want to follow in his footsteps?

I felt I had committed fraud. My parents had driven up from New Orleans to Washington, D.C. for my graduation from Howard University. The hallowed Negro institution had given me a degree I felt I hadn't earned. I had pranced through four years of college, and now I had a piece of parchment that said I was ready to face the world. But I wasn't. I didn't know what I wanted to be, and I felt I should by now. I was a nineteen-year-old college graduate, and I was still floundering. However, I did know that I didn't want to be a dentist, and I was trying to build up the courage to break the news to my father.

I had been lucky to attend Howard University at all. My high school grades were undistinguished. I had done very poorly on the college admission tests. My poor performance shouldn't have surprised me; I was only fifteen when I took the test. It was the first standardized test I'd ever seen, and I was the only black student in a large room of prospective college students. By the time I graduated from high school only Dillard University, a small black school a few blocks from our home in New Orleans, would take me.

I did little at Dillard to overcome my academic shortcomings. As an entering freshman I retook the tests and somehow did well enough to be placed in the honors program. The other freshman honors students were returning veterans from World War II. One was twenty-eight years old. The other was thirty-one. They became my big brothers on campus, but their influence was more social than scholarly.

The freedom that college gave a fifteen-year-old was something I couldn't handle very well. I spent most of my time playing whist and pinochle. The honors program gave me enough flexibility in reading and writing to get by.

I applied for a transfer to Howard University during my freshman year, and miraculously, I was accepted. I suspect that my father, who was an alumnus of the Howard University dental school, had some influence on the process, but I never asked. I was just happy to leave Dillard and get away from home. My father was also pleased. He saw my transfer to Howard as my first step in retracing the path he had blazed.

Howard University was the elite black educational institution in the years after World War II. Its undergraduate school might be challenged for status by Morehouse and Spelman Colleges in Atlanta, but Howard was the only true black university in the United States. It had medical, engineering, law, and dental schools and a full array of graduate departments.

Despite my own middle class upbringing in New Orleans, I found Howard elitist. I immediately disliked the haughtiness and pretense I encountered on campus. Knowing only the genteel traditions of my hometown, Howard was the first place I had ever been where black people didn't speak to one another when they passed. Many of the women students seemed extremely conscious of status. Some wore high heels and fur coats to class, as if they were only in college to snag a future doctor or lawyer. The men often dressed in suits and ties. This was the period about which E. Franklin Frazier wrote his classic study "The Black Bourgeoisie." Mrs. Bowen, my old high school principal, who put so much stock in appearance, would have loved the great attention paid to dress.

For the first time in my life, I became a rebel. Once again, I chose Army veterans as friends. Although they were much older than I, they seemed more sociable and down-to-earth than most of my classmates. Many came from poor backgrounds and could afford Howard only because of the GI Bill. In defiance of Howard's bourgeois atmosphere, they wore khakis and jeans to class, a style that I immediately adopted. Maybe because I was young and enamored of their style, they accepted me as a sort of mascot.

In a concession to my father, I joined his fraternity,

Alpha Phi Alpha. The Alphas were the oldest black fraternity in the country. My pledgemaster was David Dinkins, a marine veteran a year ahead of me at Howard and future mayor of New York City. The Alphas gave me a sense of belonging, and I was quite proud when the chapter elected me chaplain in my senior year—perhaps because I was one of the few brothers who didn't smoke or drink.

The challenge of pledging and completing probation to the fraternity was something of a rite of passage to manhood. The requirements of memorization, group discipline, and teamwork under pressure were good preparation for those of us who later would be part of the civil rights movement.

I wasn't much interested in academics, and my tender age was probably one reason why. Much of my energy at both Dillard and Howard went into keeping up with everyone else. As the youngest in a crowd—and at sixteen years old I usually was—I could either concentrate on my studies or run hard to keep up socially. I chose to play. Although I read a great deal on my own, my grades were barely above average. My only *A* in three years at Howard was in speech. I always found it easy to speak in public and to state my opinions. I could organize my thoughts quickly and express them coherently. I still get butterflies when I have to make a speech, but even as a student I had confidence in my ability to communicate.

I also focused my energies on athletics. I made both the swimming and the track teams. The university gave no athletic scholarships but segregation brought a bounty of great black athletes to Howard.

The track coach, Tom Hart, didn't pay me any attention until I started to beat the team favorites. For a long time I think he saw me as a restless little kid who did a lot of laughing and jumping around. When I started winning time trials, he thought my victories were accidents. When he realized my ability was for real, he was sorry that he had initially refused to give me a pair of track shoes. At that time, I was puzzled about why he never really helped me, but his attitude didn't bother me much. I was happy just to be able to perform. All the physical potential that I suspected I had in high school and during my first two years at Howard finally surfaced when my body matured in my last year at Howard. As a senior, I became the number-one dash man, and I won my events in several meets.

My success in collegiate athletics made me consider training and trying out for the 1952 U.S. Olympic Team. But that dream suffered a serious blow in my last important meet. Just before the end of the school year I ran in the annual meet of the Central Intercollegiate Athletic Conference, the association of the major black colleges. For the first time, I had the cinders kicked in my face. George Rhoden, the great Jamaican world record holder at Morgan State College, beat me badly in the 440-yard dash.

The way he beat me cast doubts on how good I really was. I wasn't as upset about losing as I was about running so poorly. The night before I had attended my fraternity dance. I didn't drink, but I didn't sleep either. I neglected the important mental preparation for such a meet. Instead, I spent a traumatic night struggling over whether to give my fraternity pin to my steady date for the year. Still, when the school year ended, I was toying with the idea of staying in shape so I'd be ready for the Olympic trials. However, the next few months would change my life forever.

All was not frivolity at Howard. We were very aware of the world outside the wrought iron gates of the university. The Korean War began in 1950, and communist troops overran Seoul at the beginning of 1951. ROTC participation was compulsory for all male students. I considered joining the marines after graduation, but fate seemed to intervene. I had broken an arm as a child, and it had been poorly set. It prevented me from holding a rifle the way a tough drill sergeant thought I should. This washed me out of the ROTC program, thus ending my deliberations about a military career.

On many evenings my friends and I would gather around the only television set in our dormitory to watch Sugar Ray Robinson fight. Robinson, unlike Joe Louis who could hardly put two sentences together, was an elegant, articulate spokesman as well as a boxer. He was one of the few blacks we could see on television who we admired.

We also watched Senator Joseph McCarthy's hearings, which had a chilling impact on many of us. The atmosphere of fear and accusation generated by McCarthy discouraged me from taking part in controversial activities at Howard.

In the early 1950s, the NAACP was winning college desegregation battles in the federal courts as it built the momentum that would lead to the watershed case of *Brown vs. Board of Education.* When I was in the sixth grade, my father had taken me to see Thurgood Marshall argue a case for equal teacher pay in New Orleans. I believed that the courts were the only way of ending segregation, but I didn't even join the NAACP at Howard. I worried that any petition I signed, any card I carried, later would come back to haunt me. That fear was driven home when we saw Jackie Robinson on television declaring how proud he was to be an American while denouncing singer Paul Robeson for his leftist activities.

Yet, even in the relatively benign segregation of Washington, D.C. we students felt our second-class status. We attended the funeral of Charles Drew, the Howard medical school professor who created the blood bank and pioneered the use of blood plasma. He died in a car crash down South, and the rumor spread through the black community that Dr. Drew had bled to death because he'd been denied admission to a white hospital. Drew's family later refuted that particular report, but we all knew that such instances were common.

Leaving campus always reminded us of our place in society. Wesley Mount, one of my closest friends at Howard, was struck by a car one Saturday as he walked to the Smithsonian Institution. The ambulance took him to black Freedman's Hospital instead of one of the two hospitals closer to the accident, which were for whites only. Wesley died. These were the facts of life of being black, and changing them seemed a remote possibility. The NAACP's landmark assault on the "separate but equal" assumption of the law would not begin until the year after my graduation, and the student civil rights movement was still some years away.

My college years ended too quickly. I graduated just as I was starting to enjoy school. I felt cheated out of an experience I was beginning to relish. I was even more disturbed that I didn't know where I was going. Just before the end of the school year, I attended the Alphas' annual dance and finally gave my fraternity pin to my girlfriend, a classmate at Howard. The gesture was traditional for a graduating senior to make, but it implied that we were very serious. I liked my girlfriend a lot, but I knew deep down that I wasn't ready for marriage.

These thoughts occupied me as my father's Oldsmobile swallowed up the miles. With each spin of the tires, I felt that I was coming closer to a confrontation with my father. When he and my mother were awake, I could feel the tension in the air. We didn't discuss my future, but I knew the moment would come. I was trying hard to screw up my courage for the confrontation. I rehearsed the dialogue in my head, but none of my imagined scenarios ended very well.

2

On
Kings
Mountain

Getting to North Carolina gave me a temporary reprieve. Our first stop was Lincoln Academy in Kings Mountain, North Carolina. The Congregational church was holding a summer conference there, and my parents wanted us to attend. Lincoln Academy was one of a string of schools built for blacks after Emancipation by the church's American Missionary Association. Lincoln Academy was a high school, but its campus looked like a small college. The low, redbrick buildings, the chapel, and the bell tower reflected the school's New England roots, but the setting atop a hill with mountains rising in the background was, emphatically, the South.

My parents had their own room at Lincoln. My younger brother was placed with some other young boys, and I shared a room with John Heinrich, a young white minister. Heinrich had been a Yale Divinity School classmate and close friend of the Rev. Nicholas Hood, our new pastor at Central Church in New Orleans. Heinrich was on his way to Rhodesia (now Zimbabwe) to serve as a missionary with his wife and newborn baby.

The commitment that I observed in John Heinrich added urgency to my own self-examination. No one at the schools I had attended ever suggested that I try to help black folk. Howard University's emphasis, and the mission of most black colleges in those days, was to better yourself and advance the race through your own achievements. None of this was sacrificial in nature. Get yourself a good job. If you're a lawyer, doctor, or dentist making plenty of money, you can then do civil rights work. So the thinking went. But here was a young white man willing to take his wife and infant child to Africa so he could help others. His commitment impressed me and made me examine my own goals and aspirations.

My parents lived through the Depression, and their first thought was for security. It usually takes at least two secure generations for people to have a sense of responsibility toward others. I was that third generation. My grandfather had been a successful businessman and a well-respected leader in Louisiana's Prince Hall Masons. My father was a dentist. I was the generation destined to make a contribution to the world at large. My contribution was to go beyond my family and include a contribution to my race and humankind.

I saw direction and destiny in the commitment of John Heinrich. I don't think it had ever been clear to me before. It was nothing he did; nothing he said. Something in his life quietly testified.

The contrast between John Heinrich's commitment and my indecision triggered my memory. I recalled the past summer when I ran into a downtrodden classmate in New Orleans. I was on duty as lifeguard at the Hardin Playground swimming pool, one of two swimming pools in New Orleans open to black youth. An older youth, looking rather haggard, dove into the deep end of the pool and went straight to the bottom. There was no struggle. He just seemed to pass out as he fell into the water. It took two of us to bring him to the surface and take him out of the pool. He was not drowning; he was high on heroin.

As he began to sober up a bit due to the cool water shock and the hot summer sun, we began to talk.

"You don't remember me, do you?" he said.

He looked strangely familiar, though, for the life of me, I could not recall who he was.

"We went to Valena C. Jones Public School together. Remember our third grade teacher?"

And then it all came back. He and I had played mumbletypeg with an ice pick in the rear of the overcrowded classroom. We were caught and sent to the principal's office. The principal sent us home to get our parents. My mother came right away, and I went back to class with only some minor punishment at home.

Lincoln, my classmate, never came back. His mother had five children and worked as a domestic worker on the other side of town. She only got paid for the five days she worked. She could not afford to come to school to see about her child. (Domestic wages were a dollar a day plus lunch and bus fare.) Consequently, Lincoln had not been back to school since third grade. He had been to reform school and Angola, the Louisiana State Penitentiary. He spoke with the wisdom and eloquence of a tough street life. He spent most of the morning congratulating me on being in college and how important a good education was if I was going to help make life better for people like him who could not get their lives together.

I was seventeen and playing my way through life, taking the future for granted. Lincoln was every bit as smart as I was and discussed his imprisonment with a level of understanding and political insight that I had not heard in my sociology courses. For the first time in my life, I knew the meaning of the phrase, "There but for the grace of God go I," and I began to recall my grandmother saying, "From everyone who has been given much, much will be demanded" (Luke 12:48 NIV).

Now I was being reminded of all these admonitions by the very presence of a young missionary.

Heinrich and I never specifically discussed what I should do with my life, but his lifestyle appealed to me. He didn't seem the least bit religious—at least not in the rigid, pious way I expected a missionary to be. We never had a conversation about God. But I saw commitment in Heinrich that I envied.

Another man who was influential in my life was at the conference. Nick Hood was still only in his twenties, but he was smart and full of enthusiasm. I had liked Nick since he had taken over as pastor of Central Church the year before. He and his wife had stayed with my parents while the parsonage was being renovated, and I got to know him when I was home that summer.

Nick's predecessor, the Reverend Norman Holmes, had been our minister for more than thirty years. The Rev. Holmes was an elderly man, extremely philosophical, even distant, in his sermons, but greatly loved in the community. He and his wife, Gertrude, were people of puritan virtue, honest, hardworking, humble, and intellectual.

Nick was a startling contrast to Rev. Holmes. A native of Terre Haute, Indiana, he had never lived in the South until he moved to New Orleans. He challenged the traditional image of a black preacher simply because of his youth. His wife, Betty, was still in college when we first met, just a year or so older than me. Nick made a great impression on me and other young people who worshiped at Central.

Nick's discipline and dedication were inspiring. He woke up at 5:00 A.M. every day to read. His sermons, delivered in a soft, high-pitched voice, were down-to-earth, straightforward, and dealt with the application of theology to the concerns of everyday life. He was not otherworldly, yet he possessed a depth of spirit that could move the congregation. Central Church was full on Sunday mornings.

Nick and I did not easily develop a personal relationship. He was very serious, and I was superficial and irresponsible. I avoided extended conversations with him, and he did not press me.

One day at Kings Mountain, a group of young men in my Bible study group decided to skip class and climb to the top of the imposing mountain peak that served as a backdrop to the school. When we reached the winding path at the bottom base of the mountain, someone suggested that we run. After a year of varsity track and swimming, I was in the best physical condition. Despite the hot summer day, I took off at full speed.

There's no more exhilarating feeling than running when your body is in excellent shape. I ran as hard as I could and reached the top of the mountain a good fifteen or twenty minutes ahead of everyone else. I felt full of that floating transcendental feeling that often comes from such exertion. I was wringing wet. I stripped down to my underwear and laid my clothes on the rocks to dry.

I looked down at the valley, and the beauty of it suddenly overwhelmed me. On that clear June day I could see for miles in every direction. The North Carolina pines were blue-green. The valley was in full bloom. The greens and yellows of the cultivated fields blended into the wild landscape. The sun shone brightly in a deep, blue sky. I saw the harmony of the valley as the harmony I longed to have in my inner being.

I had a very strong religious upbringing. My maternal grandmother was a New Orleans Creole, the daughter of a Polish immigrant who ran a shipping line. "Grand" lost her sight when I was ten years old and she was eighty-five, and until she died four years later, I read the Bible to her daily and was exposed to her deep faith and belief. She was a remarkable woman with an unshakable faith in God and God's purpose for her life. She had absolutely no fear of death. Grand had six children of her own and raised six others that she took in off the street.

My mother was superintendent of Sunday school and treasurer of the church. My father was a deacon and sang in the choir. Whenever the church doors opened, my brother and I were there. Maybe because I was force-fed so much religion as a child, I avoided it in college. I didn't go to church at Howard, but I went to chapel from time to time. I couldn't remember anything from those services but the postlude: "The Lord bless you and keep you. The Lord lift his countenance upon you." And the rich bass line: "The Lord be gracious unto you . . . Amen." I sometimes thought of the hymns I had learned in church. Occasionally, I found myself singing the old Negro spirituals in the shower at school: "Sometimes I feel like a motherless child, a long way from home," or "Nobody knows the trouble I've seen, nobody knows but Jesus."

Without being completely aware of it, I had tried to fill a spiritual void in my life at Howard. On my own I began reading Greek and Roman philosophy. I offhandedly picked up a copy of Plato's *Republic* and then came across Marcus Aurelius' *Meditations*.

My college experience was full and complex. Life was diverse with students from all over the United States, the Caribbean, and Africa in the dorm. Membership in the fraternity and competing on the swimming and track teams combined with pressures from my girlfriend, whose friends were planning marriage after graduation, and the expectations of my father kept me very busy. But it was clear to me that I was finishing college without knowing what it meant to be a man. In my mind, a man knew what life was all about and what he wanted to do with his life. I only knew what I didn't want to do. I didn't want to be a dentist. I didn't want to get married.

Suddenly, at the top of Kings Mountain, my whole life began anew. My own religious upbringing in the Congregational church, with its rational New England roots, didn't encourage sudden spiritual discoveries. We were expected to make gradual intellectual decisions about religion. Yet, if I was ever Born Again, this was the moment. A heightened awareness enveloped me. *The earth is the Lord's and I am God's child,* I said to myself. If everything else in the world was part of God's order, then I, too, must be a part of some plan of the Creator. The issues that I had wrestled with for much of the past year seemed to flow into a conscious organized pattern. I felt at one with the heavens and the earth.

Until that moment on the mountaintop, I had lived my life simply as the child of my parents. I realized then that I didn't belong to my parents, nor did I belong to myself. I belonged to something or someone beyond me—the Creator. I had been raised in the church by God-fearing parents, but I was not interested in the traditional church or ecclesiastical rhetoric. On Kings Mountain I began to think about a personal religious purpose around which I could organize my life. When the other students finally joined me on the mountaintop I didn't say anything, but from that moment I began to think of myself in a new way. I decided that purpose, meaning, and order in nature emanated from God and that the same must be true for me.

The conference ended the next day and my family resumed our trip to New Orleans. In my new state of awareness, everything around me was new and beautiful. Traveling along the road, I realized that the negative and fearful images that blacks have of the rural South often overshadow our perceptions of its beauty. I saw an attractive and peaceful land. I savored the rich green foliage that grew out of the red clay of Alabama, a state whose very name we so often pronounced in frightened tones.

The Alabama of the Klan was also the Alabama of Booker T. Washington and Tuskegee Institute, which we stopped to visit. I had heard my parents talk often about Tuskegee and Washington's struggle to create a great school. Seeing the ancient buildings built of bricks baked by the very first students reminded me of the perseverance of black Americans against incredible odds through so much of our history.

Coming down from the hills around Tuskegee and Montgomery to the basin of the Gulf Coast was like gliding to earth on an airplane. The land carved out by the giant glaciers millions of years ago stretched flat as a sheet of ice with hardly an elevation to break the monotony all the way to the sea. We drove along Route 90 through Mobile, a town set on bays and canals, and then west along the Gulf Coast into Mississippi. This was not the mythical Mississippi of frightening swamps and harsh cotton fields. Along the Gulf, Mississippi is a state of sunshine and beautiful beaches—beaches that we blacks couldn't use. When my brother, Walter, and I as young teens attended the Dryades Street YMCA summer camp in Waveland, Mississippi, not far from New Orleans, we had been warned to keep a low profile for fear of racial incidents: "Behave! You in Mississippi now!"

We drove quickly through Biloxi, Long Beach, Pass Christian, and Waveland. Soon we crossed the Pearl River into Louisiana. As we drove across the familiar Rigolets bridge into New Orleans, I felt a surge of mixed emotions. I was glad to be home, but I knew that I was closer to a confrontation with my father. We had completed the trip but had not yet discussed my future.

As we settled down in my parents' new house on Annette Street, I realized that whatever my life's work, I would never accomplish it at home. My parents had worked hard, sacrificed and saved money to send me away to school. I had acquired just enough education, training, and new perceptions to know that I could never return to their world. For the first few weeks I did nothing. The subject of my future hung heavily in the air. I made no applications to graduate school, and I was not looking for a job. I was sure Howard graduate school would accept me, but I couldn't make up my mind what to study.

It is difficult for a young person to come to the conclusion that father may not know best. For several years I had been reading Kahlil Gibran's *The Prophet* to my parents, trying to signal my independence of thought and purpose:

And he said:
Your children are not your children.
They are the sons and daughters of Life's longing for itself.
They come through you but not from you,
And though they are with you yet they belong not to you.
You may give them your love but not your thoughts,
For they have their own thoughts.
You may house their bodies but not their souls,
For their souls dwell in the house of tomorrow, which you cannot visit, not even in your dreams.
You may strive to be like them, but seek not to make them like you.
For life goes not backward nor tarries with yesterday.

You are the bows from which your children as living arrows are sent forth.

The archer sees the mark upon the path of the infinite, and He bends you with His might that His arrows may go swift and far.

Let your bending in the archer's hand be for gladness;

For even as He loves the arrow that flies, so He loves also the bow that is stable.[1]

Mother was aware of my search for a purpose for my life, but Daddy could only see dentistry. It was his blind spot.

Daddy was a very calm man who saw emotion as a weakness. He had a very strong sense of his word. Once he was stopped by a policeman after driving through a stop sign with all of us in the car. The policeman looked at his identification that said "Doctor" and asked him if he was going on a call. "No," said my dad, "we're going to the movies." The policeman offered him a half-dozen ways of getting out of the ticket, but he just wouldn't take the bait. My mother got upset, but Dad preferred to pay a fine rather than shade the truth. He felt that integrity was a person's most important asset. For him telling the truth was related to race. If you're black, he felt, you can't be just 99 percent right.

My father was driven by a need to succeed. He had no desire to be rich and famous. He viewed success as being able to get an education and a good job in order to take care of his family and save enough money so he wouldn't have to depend on anyone else.

But by the time I was twelve, I knew I didn't want to be a dentist. My father took it for granted that I would follow in his footsteps and I hadn't ever told him otherwise.

And I still could not, even after Kings Mountain.

3

Answering
the
Call

Soon after our return from North Carolina, Nick Hood asked if I would be interested in helping him drive to Texas so he could attend a church youth retreat. I was in the mood for a trip. I desperately needed to get away from the house. The retreat, sponsored by the National Council of Churches Youth Department and the United Christian Youth Movement, was at a camp in Lake Brownwood, Texas. I decided I'd go and use the trip to visit Bob Hilliard, a Howard friend who lived in nearby San Antonio. Nick suggested I drop him off and use his car since he wouldn't need it during the retreat.

The drive to Lake Brownwood turned out to be a long and lonely six-hundred-mile journey. Once we left Houston we saw fewer people and hardly any black faces. The camp was on a back road in the woods. Darkness fell, and we got lost a few times in that strange and forbidding countryside. Nick and I started to joke that this was our last ride.

We were relieved when at around nine o'clock at night we finally found the conference site. The United Christian Youth Movement was an organization of teenagers from some twenty-five Protestant denominations. Nick was the only black participant, so Jane Alexander, the conference director, and Bob Fudge, a seminary student, pleaded with me to stay. They wanted to provide an interracial Christian experience for the participants. They had fifty or sixty white students and only Nick to make it "interracial." "Nick is a great minister," they pleaded, "but we need you desperately as a participant." If I wouldn't spend the week, they asked, would I just stay a day or two?

I thought about it. It was almost midnight, and I would have had to make the long drive to San Antonio alone. After our fright getting lost in the back woods, I wasn't anxious to find my way out by myself. As I wandered about the campsite, I was also intrigued. The young whites seemed eager to relate to me. The place was beautiful and restful. I decided I would stay a while and see how I felt about the retreat.

That week at Lake Brownwood became one of the pivotal experiences of my life. Nick was in charge of Bible studies and made me read the Bible seriously for the first time in my young life. I believe to this day that Nick developed his Bible study series with me in mind, hoping to talk me into staying. In fact, the entire trip might have been a plot on his part. But the biblical passages he emphasized in his daily sessions went to the core of the issues with which I was battling:

Therefore I say unto you, Take no thought for your life. . . . Consider the lilies of the field, how they grow; they toil not, neither do they spin: And yet I say unto you, That even Solomon in all his glory was not arrayed like one of these. Wherefore, if God so clothe the grass of the field, which today is, and tomorrow is cast into the oven, shall he not much more clothe you, O ye of little faith?

(Matt. 6:25–30 KJV)

For whosoever will save his life shall lose it: and whosoever will lose his life for my sake shall find it. For what is a man profited, if he shall gain the whole world, and lose his own soul?

(Matt. 16:25–26 KJV)

Therefore do not be anxious about tomorrow, for tomorrow will be anxious for itself. Let the day's own trouble be sufficient for the day.

(Matt. 6:34 RSV)

Nick began each study with a hymn, and he then read a carefully selected scripture and commented on his selection. After that, we would take the remainder of the hour to meditate on the deeper meaning of his reading. I'd sit alone on a rock overlooking Lake Brownwood during that hour. The camp was set in the Texas hill country and had the kind of stark beauty you see in Western movies: shrubs, rocks, and tumbleweed. Until that week, I don't think I had ever sat quietly for fifteen minutes. I had never focused on developing my inner strength in any way.

The quiet time at Lake Brownwood opened the door to my life of the soul. I was amazed at the way I could sense new things and find new answers to the questions that had troubled me for so long. A quiet confidence and peace began to replace the doubt and confusion that had been with me for the past few years. Much later, I would hear echoes of that revelation when Ralph Abernathy would say: "I don't know what the future may hold, but I know who holds the future."[1] Bible verses I had heard many times suddenly had new meaning: *The peace that passes understanding* suddenly became significant. Familiar words had meaning I could now embrace, though I still couldn't understand or explain what was happening within me. I knew that a spiritual dimension of my life was awakening.

I interpreted the "lilies of the field" metaphor in Matthew 6 to mean that a living intelligence created and operates the universe. The purpose of one's life should be to get in tune with that greater intelligence. I was trying to do that. I wanted to find a role of service in the interest of a God who works for the betterment of human life—a God of loving, understanding, and forgiving; not a God of fear. Thinking of my life in terms of service gave me a new sense of self-discovery. It reinforced the flash of purpose I had experienced on Kings Mountain. Now I was developing a sense of what I must do. I was beginning to trust my inner self and let it lead me in making choices. And I was learning the rare pleasure of isolation, despite my gregariousness, in developing new powers of reflection.

Looking back, I see now that I was also looking for the psychological strength to break from the career expectations of my parents, which revolved around definitions of middle-class success: to be more successful and to be better known than your father. My new religious purpose gave me a new authority—God. The Authority was someone my parents had always said they believed in. It would be difficult for them to reject my decision to work in some area of religious service. I was now prepared, I felt, to confront Daddy and tell him I was not interested in becoming a dentist.

Later that summer, I discovered through reading that many creative people find their life's work or receive societal recognition late in life. That was a great relief to me.

It lifted the burden I felt of going through school at such a young age, which some people took to mean that I was a child prodigy.

That summer after graduation, I lost all interest in being what someone had called "a young black in the vanguard of new attainment." I had to find my own rhythm without worrying about the expectations of others. It was comforting to realize I didn't have to rush.

Growing up in the era of quiz kids and precocious children like Philippa Schuyler, the black child pianist and composer, I sometimes felt that parents were pushing their children toward some amorphous concept of success, which usually meant notoriety or media attention. I learned that Albert Einstein and Albert Schweitzer were both in their fifties when they made their mark. I decided that fifty-five was my target age. I would work steadily until I was fifty-five, and by then I would know what my contribution to life would be.

In my new state of mind, I felt many burdens lift from me. I stopped being so anxious about whether I would ever fulfill my parents' aspirations and be rich, famous, or important. I had chosen an entirely different set of values. I was beginning a journey to greater responsibility, and I welcomed it.

At Lake Brownwood the retreat participants lived in a camp with six double bunks in each cabin. Those in my cabin often lay awake at night and talked. The whites were mostly from Texas and Oklahoma, with a few from Louisiana. They all spoke with strong southern accents; they were the very kind of people I would have expected to be prejudiced. But during our talks, we all searched for ways to understand each other, to transcend racial and cultural differences. This was the first time I had such intimate contact with white youths outside the New Orleans neighborhood where I grew up. This was the first time that I had met whites who were trying to deal with the reality of racism, who were questioning what they were taught to believe. What impressed me most about this experience was that their faith was challenging them to change.

I came away from Lake Brownwood thinking that I wanted to attend a seminary and become a minister. When I shared my thoughts with Nick, he seemed a little surprised, although I felt he had been subconsciously influencing me in that direction. "Don't rush," he said. "If you make such a decision, be sure to do so at your own pace."

The flow of events in my life seemed to be driven by some grand design that summer. Soon after I got home in early July, I received a call from the youth department of the National Council of Churches, sponsors of the Brownwood conference. They were recruiting thirty young people to work as six-month volunteers in a project to organize one million young people to recommit themselves to Christ in a call to United Christian Youth Action. The Brownwood organizers had recommended me, they said. Would I be one of their field workers?

I grabbed the opportunity to escape from home again and to explore my new sense of direction. The council mailed me a railroad ticket and instructions to report to Camp Mack, Indiana for two weeks of training. Camp Mack was sponsored by the Church of the Brethren, a denomination which, like the Quakers and Mennonites, was committed to peace.

Once again, I was one of just two blacks. The other black man was Eduardo Mondlane, a student from Mozambique. A few years later he would become famous as a founder of Frelimo, the Mozambique liberation organization. Mondlane and I struck up an instant friendship. We spent a lot of time talking, exchanging ideas, and discussing the future. He was later killed by a letter bomb shortly before Mozambique achieved its independence in the early 1970s.

At Camp Mack I was exposed to the theory of nonviolence. Don Bowman, a graduate of Manchester College and a lay member of the Church of the Brethren, gave me one of Gandhi's books, which I read with great excitement. India's independence from Great Britain in 1947 had made a great impact on black Americans. Howard University President Mordecai Johnson, who had attended the independence celebration, often spoke with great passion about Gandhi and his principles. Now I was ready to absorb Gandhi's thinking. The Western tradition of "being saved" or being "made whole" dealt partly with social responsibility—especially as interpreted historically by the Congregational Church. To Gandhi, being whole meant a confluence of the spiritual, personal, social, and political. It also meant independence from colonial rule so that people could determine their own and their nation's destiny.

The political dimension of being whole appealed to me because of my black American heritage. It spoke directly to the special ethical concerns I had struggled with since my youth in New Orleans. Western Christian theology conceives of liberation primarily in personal terms. But personal liberation wasn't enough for me. I needed to see the relationship among ethics, theology, and socioeconomic liberation. I wanted to understand the destructive effects of racism as a part of a larger worldview.

My experiences at Kings Mountain and Lake Brownwood had been mystical and personal. My introduction to Gandhi at Camp Mack wove into my concept of religion and gave me a better sense of what I had to do as a black American Christian. The experiences of the summer seemed predestined. I had left Howard unsure about myself and my future. Now I was headed in a meaningful direction. I was moving, and I was excited about my life.

After my two-week training program, the National Council of Churches assigned me to Hartford, Connecticut. I lived in a dormitory at the Hartford Seminary and worked as an organizer in Connecticut and Rhode Island. I was immediately attracted to the school and to some of the students. Once again, I made friends with several veterans who were students. They were white New England Congregationalists who went beer drinking on weekends like many other college students. I didn't drink, but their behavior challenged my assumptions about how ministers should behave. They had faith without piety and that suggested a model for the kind of life I wanted to lead—with some exceptions.

I had decided at Lake Brownwood that I would not drink any alcohol. I had never smoked, and I wasn't even drinking coffee, tea, or soft drinks. I had fervently embraced the concept of the body as the temple of the spirit, and I would not do anything to defile it. That period lasted several years. Now I can look back on it and laugh at my own seriousness, but I also appreciate my effort at discipline and dedication as necessary at that point in my life.

Since I was living on the campus and liked the atmosphere, I decided to take a couple of courses at Hartford Seminary during the fall. By the time I finished my classes I became a full-time student. After six months away from home, I finally went back for that long delayed confrontation with Daddy.

The moment of truth was almost anticlimactic. I made a carefully rehearsed speech: I was not going to graduate school but returning instead to the seminary. I had a calling to service, just as he did to dentistry. I tried to point out that he was very religious and that many of his patients brought him their emotional and spiritual problems. My attempt to suggest we were on the same path wasn't very successful. As I had feared, he became furious. It was probably one of two times I ever saw him lose his cool. He started yelling that he would not pay my tuition. "I'm through with it," he said bitterly. "I'm through with it."

My father was obviously disappointed that I had rejected his beloved profession, but he was also reacting out of concern about my future economic independence. He couldn't see me supporting a family on a preacher's salary. Many black ministers in the 1950s had to hold a second job to make ends meet. I had just walked away from one of the few professions that enabled blacks to be economically at ease. However, I withstood his blast without giving up ground. I knew what I wanted to do, and nothing was going to turn me back.

I drove back to Hartford that fall in a little car, an English Ford that I purchased with all my childhood savings. I had been offered a scholarship for my tuition and went looking for work. At one point I held three different part-time jobs, as dish washer, janitor, and clerk in the seminary bookstore.

My father was not one to hold a grudge even when he was deeply wounded. It helped that a friend he respected told him not to worry about my future and that I would succeed no matter what I did.

Eventually, Daddy softened enough to start sending me money. But he never really forgave me. Years later, when I was being sworn in as the U.S. Ambassador to the United Nations, President Carter said to him, "You must be very proud of your son."

My father replied: "If he had been a dentist, he really would have been somebody."

4

Not My Will

How can we really know when God is leading us in a certain direction? This was the question most prominent in my mind through my first year at Hartford Seminary.

After that first year, I spent the summer in Marion, Alabama. I had planned to work in New York at a settlement house, but my real purpose was to continue my efforts to be an Olympic sprinter by running with the Pioneer Track Club of Harlem. I went to Marion because Dr. J. Taylor Stanley, our Southern Conference superintendent, wrote me saying that the little Congregational church in Marion was without a pastor. He told me how an active summer program for the youth of that community would help to keep them going until he could find a permanent minister.

I was upset. My plans were made to be in New York. I suspected my parents' intervention since they were good friends of Dr. Stanley's and didn't want me to be too far from home. The Pioneer Track Club in New York was a place of opportunity in the 1950s. They would not even miss me, but a little country church in Alabama would be without a program if I did not go. This was a clear calling for me since there was no one else to do this job.

So, I drove south—rather than to New York—in my English Ford.

I arrived in Marion Saturday afternoon and went to the residence of Norman and Idella Childs, the church members who were to provide my meals during the first week of my summer internship. The Childses had five grown children, and the youngest, their daughter Jean, was a student at Manchester College in Indiana, a Church of the Brethren school. She had not yet returned home for the summer, but there was evidence of her everywhere.

First I saw a Revised Standard Version of the New Testament. It was a Thomas Nelson study version that had been underlined and filled with marginal notes on many of my favorite passages.

Then I noticed a Red Cross Senior Life Saving certificate. I was not accustomed to young black women who studied the Bible seriously and who were good swimmers.

I knew Manchester College. It was a former Manchester student who introduced me to nonviolence and the teachings of Mahatma Gandhi. This was too good to be true. I began to suspect that God had plans for me now that were much better than any I could have made for myself.

Even before Jean arrived, I had decided that the Lord had sent me to Marion, Alabama to meet my wife. And her mother and father welcomed me like one of the family.

My interest wasn't all spiritual attraction, I must confess. Norman Childs was a black Clark Gable and Idella as fiery, independent, and passionate a woman as Miss Scarlet ever hoped to be. This was a wonderful family. They could only produce a wonderful daughter. I was not disappointed, and I have not been disappointed during the forty plus years since that fateful summer.

I had never met a young woman quite like Jean. There was a simple elegance about the way she did things. She was wise beyond her years, and she possessed a sense of mission about teaching in the South which impressed me more than her charm and beauty. I had known many beautiful women, but with Jean, the beauty was not just external. It was her spirit, her dedication, and her purpose to serve others which made her the "one in a million, chance of a lifetime."

Jean and I married two years later and have always felt that our union was made in heaven. We both decided that God's plan for us was greater and better than any we could make for ourselves.

For Jean and me, the most important factor in our decision to return South after my graduation from Hartford Seminary was the uniqueness of the service we might render. Our decision to go to Thomasville and Beachton, Georgia, two small but wonderful communities in the deepest South, was motivated by the fact that no one else was likely to go there. We were both children of the South who had nurtured dreams of missionary service in Africa. In fact, we had individually applied as missionaries to Angola, in southwest Africa, before we were married. The American Board of Commissioners for Foreign Mission had a policy of not sending unmarried missionaries abroad. They did not consider our applications together, since Jean applied from Manchester College, and I applied from Hartford Seminary.

By the time they realized we were a couple, we had accepted an offer from two small churches in Georgia at an annual salary of $2,280 (fifty dollars a month from Bethany Church, forty dollars a month from Evergreen, and a subsidy of one hundred dollars per month from the church conference). We have never been any happier nor freer of debt than we were during the three years we spent in south Georgia. And there is where I began my lessons in discernment.

Each human being is unique. Our fingerprints are uniquely different. The DNA molecules which compose our genetic makeup are unique, and the life experience and opportunities which come to each of us are unique. Identical twins living in the same environment develop distinctive personalities.

Is it not reasonable to assume that the plan of God includes specific, detailed, and unique plans for each and every one of God's children? Each architect and contractor has a specific plan for the materials used in constructing a house, school, or office building. Can we not also assume in faith that the Maker of heaven and earth has detailed plans for his children who are called and chosen to join in his plans? As Paul says in his letter to the Ephesians: "For he has made known to us in all wisdom and insight the mystery of his will, according to his purpose which he set forth in Christ as a plan for the fullness of time, to unite all things in him, things in heaven and things on earth" (Eph. 1:9–10 RSV).

My discernment was tested early in my ministry. We began to complete the renovation of church buildings in Thomasville and Beachton. Soon we felt comfortable with the people in both the church and community. As the church programs, especially Sunday school and the youth group, began to serve the needs of our people with some degree of success and effectiveness, I was invited to lead Bible study at an ecumenical (interdenominational and interracial) youth conference in Lakeland, Florida. The conference was being sponsored by the Youth Division of the National Council of Churches of Christ in

America and was being led by the Rev. Don Newby, with whom I had worked as a youth volunteer during my first year of seminary. In fact it was partly through his influence that I had chosen Hartford Seminary.

At the time, there were almost six hundred executive staff members within the administration of the National Council of Churches, and only Dr. J. Oscar Lee of the Division of Racial and Cultural Relations was an African American. Don Newby soon became director of the Department of Youth Work, and he asked if I would be interested in joining him in New York as associate director of the Department of Youth Work.

I was both flattered and shocked. We were quite happy in south Georgia. I was surrounded by two loving congregations. I had an active program for the youth of the community on the church playground, which we developed from vacant land adjacent to the church. I had taken our young people to summer youth conferences and on visits to Talladega College and the Atlanta University Center to encourage their higher education potential. Perhaps most important of all, I had learned from the wisdom of the elderly in Thomasville and Beachton.

However, I frankly must admit that I also went to Thomasville with my own hidden agenda. I had been reading Gandhi and the story of India's struggle to overcome colonialism without violence. I went back to the South in hopes of stirring up a similar movement among southern Negroes, as we then called ourselves. After almost three years, however, it was clear to me that no such movement would take place in Thomas County, perhaps for very good reasons.

Thomasville had been the site of Allen Normal Teacher Training Institute. This was one of more than five hundred schools and colleges established by the Congregational Church's American Missionary Association shortly after the Civil War. It helped former slaves gain some educational tools and deal with the harshness of racial segregation while maintaining their own integrity and self-respect.

Thomas County was a separate society that provided many of the necessities of cultural survival. Black people owned their own homes and a few businesses. Church life provided a rich social and cultural repository for coexisting with white society. There was a basic civility about life in this area of the South which was in part a result of the influence of northern plantation owners who owned huge tracts of land for recreation and conservation purposes. That is, they did not do any major farming which required large amounts of cheap labor and a system of uneducated white overseers who felt a need to abuse and humiliate their black workers. Everything was not perfect and fair, but life was more tolerable in Thomas County than in other parts of the South.

In 1950, black and white citizens in south Georgia at least tried to maintain fairness. One year President Eisenhower visited Secretary of the Treasury Humphries, who maintained a plantation between Georgia and Florida. The president was present for the Thomasville Rose Parade. We were impressed that Sunnyland Packing Company decorated their float with a simulated carton of eggs with twelve white children in the front carton and twelve black children in the back carton with the label, "Grade A White and Grade A Brown." This reflected the public image of "separate but equal" that the community sought to portray. Both black and white citizens participated in this fiction.

It was just such complicity that motivated Martin Luther King, Jr. to say, some years later, that "We cannot totally blame our situation, evil and unjust as it was, solely on our white brothers, for a man can't ride your back unless you cooperate by bending over. When the Negro straightens up his own back, his white brothers will fall off, and only then can we begin to know what it means to be brothers."[1]

Thomasville was far from being the Old South, but neither was it quite ready to become the New South. In my first effort at political action, I responded to an invitation from Grand Master John Wesley Dobbs of the Prince Hall Masonic Lodge, and Hubert Thomas, president of the Thomas County Business and Civic League. Dobbs and other Masons had responded to the challenge Thurgood Marshall and the NAACP had issued in the wake of *Brown vs. Board of Education* to register citizens of the rural South as voters.

For me, this was a matter of community responsibility as a Christian. How could I convince my membership that they were truly God's children if the society said that they were not fully human and certainly not accorded the rights of full citizenship? I prayed daily, "Thy kingdom come, Thy will be done on earth as it is in heaven." That meant the reign of God must come to my members in Thomasville and Beachton, Georgia. I organized a registration drive to be launched by a rally addressed by Dobbs. Things were going very well, volunteers were recruited, and churches were contacted. The black intelligentsia was enthusiastic about the new leadership I was offering.

The Saturday before our kickoff rally, Jean decided that we should drive sixty miles northwest to Albany, Georgia where there was the only Sears Roebuck department store in the region. On the way back I decided to try a short cut through Moultrie, Georgia. Just a few miles out of Moultrie, we rounded a curve in the road and found ourselves right in the middle of several hundred Ku Klux Klan members all decked out in sheets and hooded masks.

The Klan was obviously preparing to visit Thomasville,

which was about twenty miles to the south, and this was their gathering place. Fortunately, they paid no attention to us as we drove by, but my mind began to race much faster than our little Nash Rambler station wagon could travel. I had the accelerator down as far as it would go. I was most concerned about my daughter, Andrea, who was just about three months old. She was asleep in the bassinet on the backseat. I'd always felt that Jean was strong enough to deal with almost anything. She followed in the tradition of the black matriarch that was exemplified in both our mothers and grandmothers. But a helpless three-month-old baby was something else.

At this stage in my life, I was not yet committed to nonviolence. I had read Gandhi, but I'd also read Reinhold Neibuhr, Dietrich Bonhoeffer, and Paul Tillich, all of whom reacted to the Christian pacifism that took so long to recognize and combat the evils of Nazism and Adolf Hitler. Their approach was to negotiate from a position of strength. It seemed credible at the time that the Klan would be visiting us in Thomasville. John Wesley Dobbs was scheduled to drive into town from Atlanta just in time for the meeting. It was my name that was on the posters. If the Klan were going to try to intimidate anyone, it would probably be me.

At the time, we lived on the second floor of a dilapidated old house that we had renovated ourselves with help from friends and relatives from New Orleans. It had a flimsy wooden frame structure with front stairs. It was hardly safe to live in as it was. One fire bomb, or even a match lit by the Klan, and we would be in serious danger.

I developed a strategy. I would wait for them downstairs and attempt to talk with them if they came to our house. I wanted Jean to sit in the front window upstairs with our rifle. I knew she could shoot. We had once stopped in a shooting gallery on Coney Island where she hit sixteen of twenty little rabbits hopping across the gallery. I would let the leader know that a rifle was aimed at him, so it would be best that we try to reason this situation out. I really felt no fear. I believed that it was possible and necessary to try to negotiate.

Jean, however, would have none of it. She had studied with committed pacifists at Manchester College. There was no arguing with her.

"What are you here preaching about?" she protested. "Don't you believe what you preach? I'm not ever going to point a gun at another human being."

I said, "The Klan doesn't act like human beings."

"That's probably the same thing that they say about you," she replied, and repeated, "Don't you believe in what you're preaching?"

"What do you mean?" I shouted. "Of course I believe in what I preach. What's that got to do with the Klan attacking my family?"

"Well if you're going to preach about the cross and resurrection, you ought to believe that God will take care of your family."

I thought that I'd married a religious fanatic. Then it suddenly dawned on me that she was really serious about her faith in a way that most Christians never have to be.

I was still not ready to sit back and do nothing, though I was properly chastened for my lack of faith. She really did have a good point, but I believe that people ought never to court danger recklessly; we bear the cross only when there's no possible way to avoid it. I decided that it was better to leave the house and take Jean and Andrea over to the home of one of our church families.

My concern turned out to be somewhat exaggerated. The Klan did hold its meeting on the Courthouse Square in Thomasville. However, black leaders had already visited the three major power influences in town: the mayor,

Sunnyland Packing Company, and Flowers Bakery. All three had agreed that they would discourage their workers from involvement with the Klan. They also implored the sheriff to restrict Klan activity to the town square and prohibit their efforts to parade through the black community to intimidate our citizens from registering to vote.

This was my first lesson, one which I would never forget, in the influence of the business community on public affairs. This lesson served me well along the civil rights journey in Birmingham, Albany, Savannah, and later as mayor of Atlanta. The main lesson of this incident in Thomasville, however, was Jean's challenge to my faith and my preaching. Could I *really* believe in the message of the cross and the power of the resurrection? That is the ultimate question of faith. In later years I would hear Martin Luther King, Jr. issue the same challenge, time and time again: "If a man hasn't found something he's willing to die for, he is probably not fit to live."

After almost three years in Thomasville we had two wonderful daughters, Andrea and Lisa, and had formed solid friendships with the townspeople. Now we were being asked to leave behind a good life with which we were very comfortable to go to New York.

While pondering our future I went to the woods at the cottage of some friends. For three and a half days I remained alone, walking in the woods, reading, thinking, and praying about the alternatives. Should we remain in Georgia or move on to New York? Jean had no interest in moving, but she was very supportive of my decision-making process and my need to be alone while I searched for an answer. When I returned I was almost certain that I should go to the National Council of Churches (NCC) Department of Youth Work. I would be living in the North, but I would be working throughout the nation. I would work especially with young people in the South, both black and white.

Jean and I were sorry to leave the comforts of Thomasville, but we could see that the work at NCC would better further the work that we had come to understand as God's plan for us.

As I began to prepare to leave, Irving Hadley, one of the church trustees in Beachton, came to ask me if I would promise to return to perform his wife's funeral. She had been released from the hospital with an inoperable cancer. I assured him that I would do my best to return and promised to stop by their house to pay what I thought might be my last pastoral call on his wife, Leola. I was scheduled to leave for New York the next day.

When I went to visit the Hadleys, I was surprised to find Leola sitting on the front porch. We talked, prayed, and read the Bible together. She assured me that she was ready for whatever the Lord had in store for her, but that she was not going to take pain medicine anymore because it made her groggy. She had gotten up and put her clothes on and come outside because she didn't want everybody coming around feeling sorry for her. She was indeed a strong woman and so typical of the black women who had to be strong to help protect their husbands and children from the harsh realities of rural life in the segregated South.

I did my best to encourage her, but her son had already had her medical records reviewed at Sloan-Kettering Cancer Center in New York. No hope was offered. The only course of action was to take her burdens to the Lord and leave them there. This was the essence of our prayer together. I left Beachton thinking of the blessing it had been to know and work with such strong, wonderful, and loving people.

I never did get invited back for Leola's funeral. I returned to visit a year later and found her out in the yard transplanting a tree. She had rebuilt her kitchen cabinets, painted the house, and generally stepped up her activities. She was trying to get everything in order for her husband in case the Lord called her home. Miraculously, Leola lived another thirty years and outlasted her husband and her son. When she died alone in a nursing home, nobody around knew of my promise to preach at her funeral.

When Jean discovered, years later, that she had cancer, the memory of Leola Hadley's triumph came back to us with a flood of inspiration and encouragement.

I have found that when God calls anyone to a task, there is usually a larger plan of which any one person is only a small but significant part. The way is already prepared. There are problems and challenges to be faced, but these are often there to help us grow stronger. It's as though we're constantly tested and must prove ourselves worthy or at least able to bear the burdens of that particular responsibility. One of my favorite hymns, "How Firm a Foundation," says it quite well:

> *When through the deep waters, I cause thee to go,*
> *The rivers of sorrow will not thee overflow;*
> *For I will be with thee, Thy troubles to bless,*
> *And sanctify to thee Thy deepest distress.*
>
> *When through fiery trials thy pathway shall lie*
> *My grace all sufficient, shall be thy supply*
> *The flames will not hurt thee; I only design*
> *Thy dross to consume and thy gold to refine.*

I have come to understand that all of these obstacles are but a part of the divine process. God knows just how much we can bear. Just as weightlifters get stronger by increasing the weight and strain on their muscles through practice and repetition, so spiritual strengthening comes as we learn to follow the plan of God and spiritually discern the hand of God guiding our lives.

When the Lord calls any of us to a task, there is usually a moment in which everything seems to work itself out. There are problems to be faced, but the solution is near at hand. As with Abraham, God provides a ram in the bush.

5

Changing the World

Going to Sunday school can be dangerous, especially if you begin to really believe the things that you are taught. That's the only way I can explain my belief that the world can become a better place. I was taught to pray, "Thy Kingdom come, Thy will be done, On earth as it is in heaven" (Matt. 6:10 RSV). I came to believe that this was more than a pious petition for the condition of the world. It was both a call to obedience to the will of God and a call to action.

In the early years of my ministry, I read Dr. Leslie Weatherhead's book *The Will of God* and E. Stanley Jones's devotional *The Way*. During the same period I was introduced to the autobiography of Mahatma Gandhi, *Experiments with Truth*.

This was a time of great optimism. America and its Allies had won World War II and established a global possibility of peace. Conversely, in the wake of the war Europeans were very pessimistic about the perfectibility of humankind. They had firsthand experience with the failure of the church and the forces of reason to comprehend the evils of Nazism.

Americans—even Americans who knew the personal humiliation of racism—still believed that God and man together could, and would, make the world a better place. America's optimism set forth a vision of an orderly planet in which all people could be free to pursue happiness in their own way. Martin Luther King, Jr.'s dream already lived in the hearts of the people long before he articulated it in his famous "I Have a Dream" speech given in Washington, D.C. in August 1963.

Generations of African Americans believed that education, hard work, and virtue would lead to the breaking down of racial barriers. These attributes would allow each individual to climb his or her own mountain to success. But after World War II, veterans who had risked their lives to "make the world safe for democracy" were denied jobs, scholars with advanced degrees were denied the right to vote, and some millionaires still had to drive to the take-out window or go to the back door for food at local restaurants, all simply because of the color of their skin. Something had to change.

By 1954, the United States Supreme Court had declared segregation of public schools unconstitutional. This decision, known as *Brown vs. Board of Education,* was followed by a series of lesser-known cases that had systematically changed the interpretation of the law of the land, but there was little implementation and no enforcement of the law in most of the South. The continual inequities led to the formation of the Southern Christian Leadership Conference (SCLC) in New Orleans in 1956. The SCLC selected as its purpose "To Redeem the Soul of America," at the suggestion of the Reverend Joseph Lowery, a Methodist minister and civil rights leader in Mobile, Alabama who would later become president of SCLC.

The southern civil rights movement was led largely by clergy who took seriously their prophetic ministries. They believed that Jesus and the prophets were more than biblical characters to be studied and praised. The prophets and the civil rights leaders pointed to a God who cared for his children and who, "anointed [them] to preach good news to the poor . . . to proclaim release to the captives and recovering of sight to the blind, to set at liberty those who are oppressed" (Luke 4:18 RSV).

Over the past decades religion and politics have necessarily merged to inspire the human rights movements of today's world. "All men are endowed by their Creator with certain unalienable rights," states the *Declaration of Independence,* and it is the Spirit of God that empowers men and women to stand up for those rights and resist enslavement. The old Negro spiritual proclaims, "And before I'd be a slave, I'd be buried in my grave, and go home to my Lord and be free." The irrepressible human spirit, endowed by the inspiration of the Holy Spirit and the power of God, leads many to risk their lives to make the world more like the kingdom of God.

Sitting on the floor of our plush, carpeted living room in Queens, New York in the summer of 1960, we tuned our television set in to watch NBC's "White Paper" on the Nashville sit-in story. I have rarely been so moved by a television program. As my family watched, we could literally feel God calling us back to the South. Jean and I had always seen our sojourn to the National Council as a time for broadening our experiences, to later apply what we had learned to our *real* work: to change the South. If the South could be changed, we felt, then the nation would be freed of politics built on racism that kept the nation locked into a militaristic worldview and made it impossible to focus on the basic human needs of our society—education, health, and housing.

However, before we could "beat swords into plow-shares," we had to deal with the institutional structures of racism which separated men and women from their brothers and sisters, and, therefore, from God. As it says in the first epistle of John, "If any one says, 'I love God,' and hates his brother, he is a liar; for he who does not love his brother whom he has seen, cannot love God whom he has not seen" (1 John 4:20 RSV).

In the Nashville sit-in story, we watched young people of the South, inspired by the teachings of Jesus and the nonviolence of Gandhi, challenge entrenched southern customs without violence, hatred, or bitterness. The students of Fisk University, the American Baptist Seminary, and Tennessee State University set an example that students all over the world would follow. The students were helped by the Reverend Kelly Miller Smith, who pastored one of the more prominent Baptist churches in Nashville, and the Reverend James Lawson, who had served as a Methodist missionary in India. With quiet dignity, they challenged the law and practice of segregated eating facilities. When they were abused and beaten they did not fight back. When they were jailed they sang and prayed and discussed this new turning point in their faiths. Faith turned to action.

Both Jean and I knew it was time to return to the South. But we were not students. We were a family with two children and another on the way. Traditional expectations told us this was supposed to be a time of establishing our family and enjoying the comforts of our newly acquired home. But we both felt the call. How we would answer was not yet clear.

Then things began to happen. I wrote to Dr. Martin Luther King, Jr. expressing an interest in returning home.

He asked his good friend Stan Levinson to talk with me about coming to work as Dr. King's administrative assistant. I was more frightened by this offer than flattered. Martin had already been on the cover of *Time* magazine and was a respected world figure. I didn't feel as if I were ready to take on that kind of responsibility. At that time SCLC was a small operation staffed by Baptist preachers. I felt inadequate to the task of fitting in with so many outstanding leaders who had already earned their credentials by leading local civil rights movements across the South.

About the same time, I was invited to lead worship at a student conference at the Highlander Folk School in the mountains just outside Knoxville, Tennessee. Many of the student sit-in leaders from Nashville also had been invited, so I jumped at the opportunity. This visit began a turbulent chain of events that ended up with my family moving to Atlanta a few months later.

I declined the job offer with SCLC and accepted an offer to work with Highlander Folk School in their adult citizenship program, which was designed to train teachers to teach their neighbors to read and help them to register to vote. Resigning my position at the National Council of Churches was difficult. I really loved my work there, and the staff had been like a new family, one that crossed lines of race, age, sex, and denomination. It was hard to leave, but the call to the South was just too strong and too clear for both Jean and me. We felt secure about the position at Highlander as I would be a bit removed from the day-to-day crunch of action and the pressure of leadership. I also wanted to write about the movement and record this valuable moment in history from a slightly removed perspective. But, in truth, I was afraid of the burdens of leadership.

Jean was completing her master's degree thesis in education at Queens College and was expecting a baby during the same month. Fortunately, she finished the thesis on time, and Paula Jean was born a few weeks later.

We put our house up for sale and almost immediately found a buyer. Then the state of Tennessee closed Highlander and confiscated the property. The state had been receiving complaints from around the South about Highlander. Rosa Parks had attended a conference there shortly before she sparked the Montgomery bus boycott by refusing to get up and give her seat to a white man. Martin Luther King, Jr. had addressed a gathering of civil rights workers at Highlander, and the sit-in students had met there to plan their future efforts to expand the movement from the cities to the smaller towns and rural areas of the South.

None of these gatherings at Highlander was a secret. All of these meetings had been open to some members of the press, and we all knew that the proceedings were bugged by the FBI and local authorities. The movement policy was to do everything in the open; nothing was secret.

Highlander was closed on the ridiculous charge it was running a bootlegging operation. Septima Clark, a distinguished sixty-year-old schoolteacher who had been fired from her teaching position in Charleston, South Carolina for her membership in the NAACP, was now charged with supposedly carrying twenty-six gallons of moonshine out to her car in two suitcases, and Highlander was closed temporarily.

The Field Foundation had already approved funding for the citizenship program, but we now had no place to do the training. The program was to have been conducted by SCLC in cooperation with Highlander.

So there I was with a wife, two children and a newborn baby, and no house or job. Everything that had seemed to be working out so perfectly suddenly fell apart. I found encouragement in a song lyric that Tina Turner released at about the same time, "Darling, you know it's going to work out fine." I don't remember what she was singing about, but the title and the rhythm were a message from heaven. God does move in mysterious ways!

As a minister of the United Church of Christ, I was familiar with several schools in the South that educated the former slaves after the Civil War. These schools were maintained by the Congregational churches until the 1940s when most were turned over to the various state and county boards of education. Dorchester Academy near Savannah, Georgia was continued as a community center by the UCC Convention of the South and the local congregation. I went to Wesly Hotchkiss of the UCC Board for Homeland Ministries to ask if the Board would allow us to utilize Dorchester Center to conduct the citizenship program. He readily agreed and asked that I join the Board of Homeland Ministries staff and serve as the administrator of the project.

That opened the door for us to successfully make our move back to Georgia. By the fall of 1961, we had purchased a small home in Atlanta. All my reservations were now swept away. There was no hiding place, no rationalization that would allow me to deny my own sense of inadequacy and genuine anxiety about putting my family's security, not to mention my own life, at risk during this time of unrest. It was a time of testing, but God again provided the strength, energy, and insight for every decision. I was ready to take another leap of faith.

The South was becoming an increasingly dangerous place, and the movement always operated under a cloud of rumor and innuendo. Black parents became more concerned about security for their children. This was especially true in the middle-class black circles in which my family moved. It was also true in Martin's family. His parents, Mama and Daddy King, as they were affectionately called by the movement family, strongly encouraged Martin to return to Atlanta as co-pastor of Ebenezer Baptist Church. Threats on his life, the bombing of his home, and several trumped-up indictments which occurred in Montgomery made clear that the state of Alabama was determined to use its power to crush his ministry. But in spite of the fact that Georgia was no more inclined toward justice for its black citizens than Alabama, there was a stronger history of black intellectualism, black institutions, and safety for black citizens in Atlanta.

Martin returned to Atlanta to become co-pastor of Ebenezer Baptist Church with his father. Atlanta offered much in the way of support. The established church base and the powerful influence of Martin's father in local politics created for him an island of security in the turbulent Southern sea of racism and violence in which he chose to work.

My family also enjoyed a measure of safety in Atlanta. A strong black community protected the civil rights movement from the kind of capricious abuse and physical harm to which we might have been subjected in smaller towns across the South.

Atlanta also offered the presence of six historically black colleges in the Atlanta University system and a newspaper whose editor, Ralph McGill, was one of the few prophetic white voices calling for liberty and justice for all in the South. Fortunately, we had learned that we could trust our heavenly Father to lead us even through "the valley of the shadow of death" (Ps. 23:4 KJV).

Over the next four years the Citizen Education Project trained more than a thousand local leaders from east Texas to Virginia. In the process we planted seeds of faith and freedom that bore much fruit over the next few decades and, indeed, changed the face of the South.

With Septima Clark and Dorothy Cotton, I toured the

South, looking for "Ph.D. minds" among people systematically deprived of an adequate education because of racial discrimination. Among our first recruits was Fannie Lou Hamer, future heroine of the Mississippi Freedom Democratic party and inspiration to the entire nation due to her courage, determination, and strength of spirit. Mrs. Hamer's expression, "I'm sick and tired of being sick and tired," was a cry for justice from a woman who had picked cotton and sharecropped most of her life.

In 1961 Mrs. Hamer was the timekeeper on a plantation near Ruleville, Mississippi, a job that she'd held for more than a decade and had earned by her integrity and obvious leadership ability. But when she came to Dorchester Center on a bus loaded with Mississippi leaders to be trained in methods of teaching literacy and registering voters, she returned home to find that her belongings had been removed from her sharecropper cabin and placed out on the highway. The plantation owners thought they were evicting her and making her an example to frighten others, but they actually set her free. Millions of Americans saw Mrs. Hamer testify on live television during the Democratic National Convention. She became one of our best organizers. Our initial forty dollars per month stipend was later raised to sixty dollars per month, allowing her to move into a small house in Ruleville and begin a new life.

Things never got easier for Mrs. Hamer, but she never wavered or despaired in spite of her trials and suffering. She chose to challenge the system and did so with a calm determination.

In 1963, during the Birmingham movement, we scheduled a planning meeting for Dorchester. Fannie Lou Hamer and Annelle Ponder of the SCLC staff were representatives from Mississippi. On their return to Mississippi via Greyhound bus they stopped in Winona, Mississippi and went to use the rest room. This was more than two years after President Kennedy's executive order to the Interstate Commerce Commission declaring that *all* facilities be available to *all* travelers.

Nevertheless, the group was arrested and taken to jail. We learned of this the next morning when the bus arrived in Greenville, Mississippi without them. Lawrence Guyot, the project director of the Student Nonviolent Coordinating Committee (SNCC), rushed over to bail them out only to be thrown in jail himself. The next night, Medgar Evers, the NAACP state director, was assassinated in Jackson, Mississippi. It seemed as though the whole state might explode in violence. James Bevel, the SCLC representative in Mississippi, and I decided that we would go over to bail the group out of jail. The only problem was that we didn't have a car, so we went to borrow Dorothy Cotton's car.

Dorothy is a wonderful woman with a great spirit. But she was indeed a woman, and our chauvinist attitudes said that you didn't take women into dangerous situations. That night we discovered that Dorothy was a feminist long before there was a National Organization for Women. She refused to give us her car. In fact she was furious and said, "I don't need you all; I'll go get them out of jail by myself." Realizing we had an unreasonable female on our hands, Bevel and I jumped into the car as Dorothy drove out of Birmingham toward Mississippi at speeds in excess of ninety miles per hour. Every time we suggested that she slow down, she shouted, "I don't need you to tell me how to drive. You men make me sick!"

Shortly after we crossed into Mississippi and began to travel a stretch of two-lane roads, our car crested a hill. With Dorothy still doing ninety and fussing at our chauvinism, we looked up only to see two eighteen wheelers side-by-side, coming up the hill toward us.

For ten seconds that seemed like a lifetime, we looked death square in the face. At the last minute, Dorothy, who really was a good driver, swerved off the highway and just barely missed a head-on collision. She pulled over and let me drive. All of us were shaking as a result of our near brush with death.

It was then that I thought of Albert Camus, the French existentialist writer who wrote about the absurdities of life. Camus, himself, was killed in his prime in a meaningless automobile accident. My companions and I had all been very much afraid of what might await us at a Mississippi jail in the wake of the Evers assassination, and our earlier emotional clash really had been an attempt to fight our own fears. But in the aftermath of a senseless near-accident that might have killed us all, we finally relaxed and began talking about our fears.

All of a sudden Medgar Evers' martyrdom in the cause of freedom seemed like an honor. Death is inevitable. We are fortunate if we are able to contribute to the values and ideals of our lives even in the act of dying. Martyrdom has always been one of the powerful mysteries of life. To die in a cause for which you truly believe is a blessing, for you contribute to that cause far beyond the physical act of death.

Martin King often quoted Reinhold Niebuhr who had said, "It is better to die for a cause that will ultimately succeed, than to live for one that will ultimately fail."

We were all so thankful to have escaped a meaningless death in a traffic accident that we began to think anything that happened to us at the Winona jail would be a blessing. The next hour of driving, now within the speed limit, was one of the most inspiring of my life. We talked openly of death without fear and began to discuss the power of the cross. We began to see that God had changed the world through the shedding of innocent blood. It often takes the courageous death of an innocent human being doing the right thing, in the right place, at the right time, to mobilize the "coalition of conscience" that changes the world and takes human history to higher levels. Death is an inevitable part of life to be embraced rather than feared.

When we arrived at the jail we met a deputy sheriff, who was somewhat hostile toward us but not violent. The sheriff was on the phone when we walked in and shortly he looked up and asked, "Who is Andy Young?" then handed me the phone. It was Wiley Branton, the director of the Southwide Voter Education Project. Wiley was from Arkansas and maintained an Arkansas twang, a speech pattern that sounded more southern country than black. I'm sure the sheriff thought that he was talking to a white federal official. The sheriff immediately began to shuffle papers and tell us where to sign the bonding proceedings for the release of Mrs. Hamer and the others.

As they began to come from their cells they were happy but very bruised and battered after almost a week in jail. They had been beaten repeatedly for refusing to say "yes sir." These were polite and gentle souls, but they refused to be intimidated. When the jailers couldn't break their spirits, they had begun to attack their bodies. I was enraged, but the sweet and dignified countenances of Annelle Ponder and Fannie Lou Hamer reminded me that hatred was too great a burden to bear.

James Bevel put our outrage into perspective when he said that we had to become "political psychiatrists" and view our oppressors as our patients. "A psychiatrist doesn't get angry with his patients when they are violent towards him; the doctor must help his patients to realize that their violence grows out of sickness and insecurity. We must help them, not hate them."[1]

That was fine theoretically and even theologically, but

we were dealing with the systematic abuse of authority with the specific intention of enslaving citizens through fear. This entire system had to change. Racial discrimination and domination were not just the problems of a few individuals; an entire social order created this situation. That social order had to be changed.

So many of America's problems were anchored in racism. Even after President Kennedy's election, the appointment of federal judges for the entire nation was under the control and influence of Senator James Eastland of Sunflower County, Mississippi. That very county had refused to let Fannie Lou Hamer vote and had denied voting rights to the majority of its citizens who were black.

Senator Eastland had an influence on judges appointed from New York to California. To get a judge confirmed by the Senate Judiciary Committee some political deal had to be made which extended racism's hold on our body politic. Since racism's base was in the rural South, the deals made usually indirectly hurt the rapidly growing cities of America, by concentrating political favors in the southern rural states. Eastland's influence all but assured that the most conservative judges were the ones nominated, north or south.

Many of the current problems plaguing the urban infrastructure in metropolitan areas are the result of rural, racist domination of the U.S. Senate for almost half a century. To free America, to free the cities, black people had to be freed and guaranteed the right to vote.

In the early years of the civil rights movement black America was not yet strongly focused on the vote as the key to their salvation and the liberation of the nation. The daily humiliations—denial of rest room facilities and refusal of service at the lunch counters and restaurants—initially dominated the agenda of civil rights groups. The very department stores that sold blacks clothing, furniture, appliances, and toys for our children would not sell us a sandwich or allow us to sit down for a comfortable lunch with a friend as white customers could. These daily humiliations were more evident and more outrageous in the minds of many. These problems were what captured the imagination of the people.

The civil rights groups were never really made up of organizations where people sat down and planned long-range strategies and adhered to them. These were people movements where people like Rosa Parks or the students of Greensboro and Nashville got ideas and took action. Only then did organizations and leaders come along, interpret those actions, and garner national, political, and financial support. Individual acts of conscience, motivated by some crisis or incident or by some deep-seated spiritual inspiration, convinced us that God was showing us a way to change the world. Even when we could see no human way that we could realistically challenge the racist power of the South and the nation, we felt the spirit leading us on.

6

Breaking Down Walls

It seems as though I've always been different, always in the minority. I grew up in a neighborhood where most of the children were white. I went to school at the all-black Valena C. Jones Public School where I was considered middle-class. Most of the students came from very poor families. My family's social relations were with the all-Catholic Creole population, and we were Protestant. In college I was young, starting at fifteen when most of the men were returning veterans of World War II and in their twenties or thirties. In the civil rights movement, most of the preachers were Baptist, and I was a Congregationalist (United Church of Christ).

All through my life it has been necessary for me to chip away at the various kinds of walls that people built to exclude anyone who is the least bit different. Now as a world community, the extremes of ethnic warfare, ethnic cleansing, genocide, and many variations of tribal and gender conflict threaten to destroy any sense of community, state, and nation around the world. Breaking down the walls that divide us has become essential to the survival of the human race. In fact this is one of the clearly stated ministries of Christ. The letter to the Ephesians describes the ministry of reconciliation, according to the purposes of God: "For he is our peace, who has made us both one, and has broken down the dividing wall of hostility" (Eph. 2:14 RSV).

Oppression breeds a certain amount of stoicism. When anyone does not have many avenues of redress or the power to defend oneself and family, the stoic response is to bear up gracefully and assume an air of rising above the suffering through the power of one's mind and spirit. This was the approach I saw my father take. He never seemed to let anything touch him. He was always a man of reason, and he taught me never to lose my cool. His advice was a marked contrast to the admonition of Joseph P. Kennedy to his children, "Don't get mad, get even." My father's advice was, "Don't get mad, get smart."

My father was almost always forgiving and nonviolent in relation to his antagonist. I asked my first question about race after I had been told that I could not sit in front of the bus because only white people could sit there.

In New Orleans in the 1930s the streetcars required that "colored patrons" sit behind a screen. My parents went to great lengths to help me accept this reality without a sense of inferiority, but it was very difficult for a preschool child to comprehend the foolishness of segregation. In New Orleans centuries of mixed relationships have produced a population that is beautifully blended. I couldn't understand just what it meant to be white or black. Yet the law required that some be considered white and others Negro. In my young eyes all people were colored various shades of pink, beige, brown, or black.

It was quite confusing and illogical to a preschool child,

and I often embarrassed my parents by openly asking about anyone we might meet, "Is he white?" This "white" status was quite a thing to understand.

My father gave a long and detailed explanation of race and skin color, but he also assured me that we are all children of one loving, heavenly Creator, even though we are all somewhat different.

My father's concept of "getting smart" meant that one should think one's way through any difficulty or challenge. Anger only paralyzes the thought process and takes away one of a person's unique strengths. Animals are given to fight or flight, but human beings have the capacity to rise above any situation through the power of the mind and the spirit.

To reinforce this lesson my father would shadow box with me. As long as I was controlled and disciplined in my approach, he would encourage and congratulate me. Whenever I began to get frustrated and swing wildly, he would tap me lightly but persistently on the cheek and say, "That's one knockout, two knockouts, three knockouts. How many times are you going to get knocked out before you learn to control yourself and think?"

Throughout my childhood I was never in the right neighborhood. I grew up in the center of town, went to elementary school downtown, and attended high school uptown. I always seemed to be challenging somebody's attitude or power with my own ideas, though it was mostly a strategy born of the need to defend myself, to survive.

Because I was always different, younger, and smaller than most of my friends and playmates, I learned that an aggressive approach worked more often than not. I learned to reach out in friendship rather than to shrink in fear. The struggle to survive in the neighborhood and at elementary school sharpened my negotiating skills then and in my adult life. It also paved the way for my later involvement with the movement for nonviolent social change. Years later negotiating with hostile parties under United Nations auspices or attempting to prepare the way for a nonviolent civil rights confrontation were not nearly as frightening as dealing with the schoolyard bully or a gang of potentially threatening youth from another neighborhood.

None of the kids in Jones School liked the school lunch, so many passed it up and went across the street for the 1940s version of junk food. I was the one that everybody expected to have money, and many of the bigger boys thought a kid my size would give up his money or get beat up. I soon learned that I could organize several of my peers, including a few of the older and bigger boys, and if we pooled our money, we could buy a loaf of bread for eleven cents, a nickel's worth of bologna, and as many R.C. colas and moon pies as we had pennies for. Then everybody ate a pretty good lunch. My scheme became a schoolyard version of the feeding of the five thousand, though its roots were more practical than sacramental.

Learning to think and learning to share, which are two basic values of any society, also proved to be effective ways of coping with violence. The violence born of the resentment of privilege in the face of widespread poverty is characteristic of many of the geopolitical problems we face in today's world. Serious thinking and sharing were the basis of the Marshall Plan, which financed the reconstruction of Japan and Europe after World War II. Utilizing these lessons in the current struggles of modern Asia, Africa, and Central America would not be wasting energy.

The most challenging problems of my childhood perhaps were related more to class than to race. Being the son of a dentist and a schoolteacher gave me considerable advantages over most of my playmates, black or white. My problems at school with poorer black youth were more physically dangerous and demanding while the problems of race in my neighborhood were also potentially emotionally damaging.

Fortunately, my parents understood the dangers of race and worked to shelter and protect me from them even as they prepared me to deal with them in a thoughtful and rational way. At school I was on my own to cope and survive or be seriously crippled socially. This took all my interest and energy. Studies were always secondary concerns in my mind after survival, sports, and girls. Success in studies satisfied my parents, but they loved me no matter what. It really didn't matter to me what teachers thought; they were just doing a job. They didn't really care about me—except for Mrs. Ethelyn Jones Acox. (She put her arm around me one day and congratulated me on the way I formed my letters. I've been writing almost like the penmanship book ever since!)

I believed that I could always read what I needed to know. Fortunately, my parents had given me a set of encyclopedias, and I looked up anything I was interested in. The real challenge for me in school was breaking down those walls that separated me from my classmates and playmates. Class and race, though I never thought of my struggles in those words until high school, were ever-present clouds hanging over everything.

Looking back, I can now see the hand of God using these childhood challenges to prepare me for my later life as an ambassador, negotiator, reconciler, and minister to the oppressed. I have never been in a confrontation as an adult, whether with the Klan in Florida, an angry mob in Chicago, a berserk and frightened police officer, North or South, or the supposedly communist terrorists with whom I negotiated at the United Nations that were as much a threat to my personal safety, security, and sanity as the kids at Valena C. Jones Public School in New Orleans. Nothing has ever frightened me more than the gangs through whose territory I had to pass going to football games at Xavier University stadium in Gert Town or the Irish, Polish, German, and Cajun kids with whom I grew up.

Through the experiences of my life, I have come to believe that people in every situation can respond to reason. Any enemy can become a friend through understanding and problem solving. If an enemy solves his or her problems, you won't have a problem. Kids fight out of frustration, lack of confidence, and low self-esteem. I learned to always respect and watch my enemies. Much of the same truth can be applied to nations, tribes, and creeds. Nations, after all, are run by "big kids" who are still struggling with their childhood insecurities and phobias.

Growing up in a culturally diverse neighborhood is good training for life. After all, in the new global community forming at the end of the twentieth century, most people now live in neighborhoods made up of many different types of people. The earlier in life that one learns to cope with such diversity, the better off he or she is. The big problem with differences between people is that they inspire fear of the unknown. As we begin to learn more about people, we have much less to fear. There is much more that even the most divergent among us have in common than that which divides us. This is why school integration, with all of its problems, is good for all concerned. It exposes the minority youth to a majority population that they learn is human rather than superior. Minorities are often stereotyped as a means of enforcing separation, and close interaction with another race helps the majority youth to realize that they need not fear or be overcome by all those stereotypes.

The recent violence and tension in Los Angeles is an indication that racial problems cannot be ignored. Festering sores of racism and poverty breed alienation and nihilism which usually result in self-hatred and random violence. This is the root cause of black-on-black crime that now plagues America's cities. Then when some incident such as the Rodney King beating by police occurs, the whole tinder box explodes and shatters any illusion of racial harmony.

Race and ethnic relations must be addressed continuously. The leadership of the churches of the sixties was an important moral and religious influence on our racial attitudes and actions. We made racism illegal, but we didn't continue to deal with the moral and spiritual questions of feeding the hungry, clothing the naked, and healing the sick. The incidents in Los Angeles have more to do with economic justice than racial justice. Appreciating the challenge of diversity and working for the unity of humankind remain our challenge.

We have been through the process of racial unrest for almost a century in the United States, but we now see the resurgence of ethnic strife in the former Yugoslavia, with violence in Serbia, Croatia, and Bosnia erupting volcanically from tensions buried over several decades. The lesson here is not that these tensions are insoluble but that they must be dealt with openly and democratically by each and every generation. They cannot be suppressed by force without future peril.

My work in New York with the National Council of Churches Division of Youth Work gave me firsthand experience in dealing with the problems of seeking unity amid diversity. I worked with 225 Protestant and Orthodox Christian denominations which sought to preserve a level of historical, doctrinal, and cultural integrity while seeking to discover a basis for unity with other denominations. We learned that there can be no effective unity without knowing, understanding, and appreciating the nature and extent of diversity. Baptists might say, "Our ancestors *died* because of the belief in believer's baptism. We can't just ignore a tradition so sacred." And once you knew and understood their position, it was a lot easier to understand, respect, appreciate, and be tolerant of their point of view.

Each and every one of these religious groups had emerged from the struggles and sufferings of their ancestors and their efforts to establish freedom of religion in the European context of the Reformation. Now in the American situation where diversity of religious opinion is both accepted and respected, each group had to learn to express and affirm its unity with other Christians, without glossing over real historic differences. The requirement was to affirm our unity while celebrating our differences, even as we celebrate the symphony of color in a field of flowers.

In accepting this challenge in church and in society, the National Council of Churches tended to attract to its staff people of enormous sensitivity and compassion. They were indeed the most tolerant and liberal group with whom I have ever been associated. (I use "liberal" in the classic sense of believing in change without violence.) In a world where change is inevitable and continuous, the need to achieve that change without violence is essential for survival. Too few people have heard of Dr. Roswell Barnes of the Federal Council of Churches; Eugene Carson Blake, staff clerk of the Presbyterian Church; Truman Douglas of the United Church of Christ; Kenneth Maxwell of the American Baptists; Robert Spike of the United Church of Christ; or J. Irwin Miller of the Disciples of Christ, who led the churches in the postwar period. They each had an integral role in the changes which made for peace and progress in the 1950s and 1960s.

These were men of vision and commitment who helped the world to overcome the ravages and hatred of World War II and who helped to shape the world as we know it through the eyes of faith.

The Marshall Plan of the post-World War II period and the civil rights legislation of the 1960s laid the cornerstones of the present era. With the active involvement of the religious community, led by Protestants but also including Roman Catholic, Greek Orthodox, and Jewish leaders, a world emerged that was able to stem the expanse of communism and promote the development of human rights and equal opportunity for the black minority at home. The women of the world and the emerging nations that were coming of age would benefit as well from these changes. And the groundwork was laid more than a hundred years earlier by Christian missionary teaching and preaching.

For me personally, the National Council of Churches was a laboratory which immersed me in a world which was largely white, Anglo-Saxon, and Protestant. It also introduced me to the world in a new way. I was involved with Europeans and Africans in the Program to Combat Racism. My associates Don Newby, John Wood, and Wilson Cheek shared with me the insights gained in their travels and their meetings with religious leaders: Orthodox, Pentecostal, Baptist, and Jewish in Asia and the then Soviet Union. I was also involved in representing North American churches in consultation with leaders of Central and South America.

Equally as important to my future was my association with Al Cox and CBS on the television program "Look Up and Live," a weekly religious broadcast that attempted to reach out to youth in familiar language and cultural forms.

During my four years in New York with the National

Council of Churches I was not only breaking down walls in my own life, but I was developing the knowledge and understanding that would enable me to view life from the eyes of faith. I began to see the world as the whole household of God. I gained the perspective of ecumenism. I also began to appreciate television and how it could shape history in times to come.

As associate director of the Department of Youth Work, I served as a consultant to the denominational youth departments on theology of youth, youth culture, and human relations. My work involved me with young people from the South and from northern suburbs. My ministry was not primarily about social change; I was to help these young people grow in grace and understanding of the world in which they would live and lead. I learned that many of the problems I had experienced as a young African American in a segregated society were also tormenting young people from the privileged white families of our nation. It became clear to me that we were all perplexed by a human dilemma: Life without God is lonely, alienated, and often purposeless. As a nation our problems reflect our spiritual condition more than our social or political situation. While social and political situations are very important, lasting global answers must be derived from a spiritual understanding of the human situation.

During this time I exchanged letters with young people of America's most privileged families. These letters could have been written by youth in poverty, for their poverty was a poverty of spirit rather than material things. As I read these letters, I was often reminded of the words of Jesus at the time of his temptation, "Man shall not live by bread alone, but by every word that proceedeth out of the mouth of God" (Matt. 4:4 KJV).

A few years later, in Birmingham, Alabama the relationships I had formed in Christian youth work opened the doors to negotiations with the Birmingham business community. Peggy Horne, whom I had met through my work with NCC, introduced me to Bishop Murray of the Alabama Diocese of the Episcopal Church, and he in turn convened meetings between Dr. Martin Luther King, Jr. and members of the Birmingham business community. It was these negotiations and the confidence that more united us as children of God than divided us racially and economically that led to the successful negotiations in Birmingham, and this eventually to the Civil Rights Act of 1964. Those earlier student contacts also began to bear fruit around the world as the struggle for human rights and human dignity encircled the globe.

My friendship with Dr. Eduardo Mondlane who founded the liberation movement in Mozambique dated back to my student delegate days at Camp Mack, Indiana. A decade later, in the 1960s as Mozambiquan citizens marched nonviolently in quest of the right to vote and majority rule, Portuguese soldiers opened fire with machine guns. That effectively ended their attempts at independence without violence. But, though they then turned to the Russians and Chinese for weapons to defend themselves in their struggle, I always remembered that the foundation of their desire for freedom and their education in the values of human rights had come from their association and education by Christian missionaries.

In 1960 I also made my first visit into what was then East Berlin through NCC and met with church youth leaders of the Lutheran Church in the then German Democratic Republic. At that time such an environment of suspicion and hostility existed that even the singing of Negro spirituals in a worship and Bible study program aroused fears that those present might lose their scholarships. "Go Down Moses" and "Oh Freedom" have always held subversive potential in an oppressive situation. The lyrics, "Tell old Pharaoh to let my people go" or "And before I'd be a slave, I'd be buried in my grave and go home to my Lord and be free," did not read like "the opiate of the people" or pie-in-the-sky religion when it appeared in a state secret police report.

My life has been full of fortuitous coincidences. Everything that has happened to me seems as though it were being coordinated by divine intelligence. I have only to be sensitive and obedient, to avoid being overly anxious, and to do the best I can with today's assignment. I can do these things knowing that the God who led me yesterday is with me today, and will guide me to my task for tomorrow.

Break down the walls that divide people. Get to know those who are different. Work to understand and appreciate others—even when they are your enemies in the present scheme of things. This is what we must do. Maintain the faith that a common ground of humanity ties us together. As Martin Luther King, Jr. was fond of saying: "All men [and women and children] are bound together in a single garment of destiny, we are woven together in an inescapable network of mutuality."[1]

7

Building Leaders

In 1963, nobody in the South was more resistant to change than the government officials of Birmingham, Alabama. It was hardly the place you'd want to thrust demonstrators who were not quite sure of themselves. But like most social change movements, we did not choose the people, the times, or the places; they chose us. And Birmingham was the scene of the first very big confrontation, the place where the civil rights movement in this country began.

Martin Luther King, Jr. was just settling into his pastorate at the Ebenezer Baptist Church in Atlanta. Reluctantly, SCLC had gone into the Albany movement in south Georgia shortly after the confrontations in Montgomery, Alabama and Jackson, Mississippi over the Freedom Rides. These movements were begun and managed by the Student Nonviolent Coordinating Committee (SNCC) and the Congress of Racial Equality (CORE).

While still working with the Dorchester Citizenship

Education Program, I helped add a few staff members to SCLC. Though we were officially a literacy training program staff, Septima Clark, Dorothy Cotton, and I comprised almost half the total SCLC staff in Atlanta. In fact, SCLC had fewer than a dozen employees nationwide, and several of these were fundraising in New York and lobbying in Washington. We were hardly the kind of force to tackle the citadel of southern segregation.

The Reverend Fred Shuttlesworth was the leader of the Alabama Christian Movement for Human Rights, the SCLC affiliate in Birmingham. Fred had been harassed, beaten, jailed, bombed, and generally abused in the press, all because he wanted his children to get a decent education in a racially integrated setting. More than fifty newly purchased homes of black citizens had been bombed simply because they were modest, single-family homes with trees, lawns, and other amenities associated with white home ownership. No one was arrested. A black man walking home from work had been castrated, and there seemed no other motive for the crime than the sick sense of sexual inferiority that his attackers harbored. Birmingham was a terrible place.

However, Birmingham was also a city with a small core of dedicated young ministers in some of the larger Baptist, Methodist, and Pentecostal churches clustered near the center of town. A. G. Gaston, one of the few black millionaires, owned a motel, insurance company, funeral home, and business school in Birmingham. Birmingham was home to a black population that had experienced some of the fruits of the industrial age in contrast to most of the South that was still essentially built around an agricultural base. Birmingham blacks had the benefits of the steel industry and organized labor. None of these characteristics would have led us to elect Birmingham as the movement town to crack the South. Rather, it was the stubborn determination of Fred Shuttlesworth who insisted that either the SCLC national office join him, or he would move on alone.

Everybody was afraid of Birmingham, though no one spoke of fear. Martin was great at turning fear into laughter. One night, as soon as it was apparent that we would be moving into Birmingham soon, he began to humorously speculate about who might have to give their life for freedom. Though we all knew that he was inevitably the prime target, he proceeded to go around the room and preach a brief satirical eulogy for each of us, emphasizing our individual foibles and foolishness. Before long, everybody was laughing and adding to the satirical commentary.

Once we got started, the Birmingham movement was really exciting. Wyatt Walker, who was then SCLC executive director, developed a battle plan we would follow shortly after the election of a new mayor in March. James Bevel, Dorothy Cotton, and I began quietly to recruit and train young people. Wyatt also attempted to organize support among the Baptist Ministers Conference, the organization representing four hundred black Baptist churches in the city, but they refused to endorse the movement or formally interview Martin Luther King, Jr.

White ministers placed a full page ad in the Birmingham *Herald,* denouncing Martin and SCLC and blaming us for causing racial problems. Everybody reacted against change but the working black people.

Martin confidently pushed ahead with nightly mass meetings that were held in the few churches open to us around town. A significant nonviolent movement was soon underway.

After several weeks of demonstrations, with twenty-five to fifty members being arrested daily, we had several hundred demonstrators in jail. The property bonds organized from black homeowners by John Drew, a longtime friend of the King family, had run out. A delegation of distinguished black leaders visited Martin in his room on the second floor of the Gaston Motel. They were from the local citizens' committee that supported us when we began. Now they appealed to Martin to call off the demonstrations and admit that racism in Birmingham was too entrenched to respond to nonviolent action.

These civic leaders asked Martin to go on a speaking tour up North to tell the Birmingham story and raise funds to get the rest of the demonstrators out of jail. Maybe at a later time, he might come back to Birmingham after some other "easier" places changed. They had little confidence in nonviolence, and though there was a great deal of admiration for Martin personally, there was no hope that he could get Birmingham to change. *The Birmingham Manifesto,* a list of objectives defined by the Alabama Christian Movement for Human Rights, expressed their reason for launching demonstrations:

To integrate lunch counters,
To hire black citizens for clerical jobs,
To speed up school desegregation, and
To allow black citizens to register to vote without delays, harassment or intimidation.

In the spring of 1963, these seemed like revolutionary demands, and the entire white community of Birmingham was aligned against us. Now, even the black leadership was losing heart and ready to give up. This was a critical juncture in Martin's development as a leader.

After listening attentively for almost an hour, Martin expressed his disappointment over the failure of many people to respond, including the Kennedy Administration. During the Freedom Rides in 1961 when black and white students tested the desegregation of bus terminals across the South, Bobby Kennedy moved decisively against the southern states' refusal to protect the Freedom Riders. Now southern states were learning to restrain Klan violence and allow the police to be the enforcers of segregation.

Martin excused himself and went into the next room alone to pray over their recommendations. In the meantime, demonstrators from the Sixteenth Street Baptist Church were getting ready. Martin had been scheduled to join them with a small group of younger pastors. Our original plan had called for a massive demonstration of the clergy about this time, but no such courageous cadre of Christian soldiers had been forthcoming. When Martin returned to the room where the leaders awaited him, he addressed them very humbly and apologetically.

"Gentlemen," he began, "I understand and sympathize with your concerns for the people in all this and for my safety as well as the success of this movement. You may well be right. Birmingham may be too tough for the level of nonviolent action and commitment that we have demonstrated thus far.

"But I would find it very difficult going around the country explaining our failure and asking people to contribute to bailing us out of a horrendous miscalculation. I have decided that the only morally defensible position I have is to continue our demonstrations as planned and join our people in jail."

With that brief testimonial he put on his denim work jacket. This was not only the uniform of Birmingham's workers, it was a symbol of the "Don't shop where you can't work" movement that encouraged black Birmingham to buy no new clothes for Easter as a part of an economic withdrawal campaign.

Joined by his younger brother, Rev. A. D. King, and

Ralph Abernathy, Martin proceeded to the Sixteenth Street Baptist Church and began a walk toward city hall. Less than two hundred yards from the church, the fifty-five demonstrators were stopped by the police. As they knelt in prayer, they were placed under arrest.

This short walk in Birmingham began the long march toward human rights in the twentieth century.

Martin's willingness to make a decision to push ahead, even when the results were impossible to predict or anticipate, was a critical element in his leadership development. It was a carefully thought through leap of faith. Martin chose to trust in the power of the spirit when all the political and social calculations seemed bleak. Only after the fact did I realize that our Birmingham day of decision in 1963 was Maundy Thursday, the day on which Jesus faced the cross.

Martin's arrest left me in the streets with several thousand infuriated bystanders. The police refused to allow Martin and his small band of demonstrators to even walk on the sidewalk to city hall. Amid the taunts and jeers of the boisterous but nonviolent crowd, the police began to panic. We had done a pretty good job of convincing the people that violence played into the hands of police and gave them license to kill people at random.

But Bull Conner, the Birmingham police chief, was not accustomed to anyone challenging the authority of his police force. Within a few minutes, while we were trying to calm and disperse the crowd with our nonviolent marshalls led by James Orange, a 6'4", 265-pound gentle giant, out came the police dogs and fire hoses. Then pandemonium broke loose. People were screaming, dogs were barking, fire hoses were sprayed directly at people with such force that it knocked them to the ground.

Finally, our marshalls began to regain a little control, and we led people back to the Sixteenth Street Baptist

Church. Soon Dorothy Cotton and Carlton Reese, the choir director for the Alabama Christian Movement, were leading the packed church in singing an old Negro spiritual, "Over my head, I see freedom in the air, There must be a God somewhere."

Then Dorothy turned to me and said, "Andy, you've got to say something."

"Say what?" I said. I had never been called on to speak at the rallies and mass meetings. There were so many great Baptist preachers, it never occurred to anyone that I should speak. I never gave a thought to how I might address or motivate a crowd, particularly a crowd that was clearly in a crisis. But all the great preachers had gone to jail with Martin. There was no one left to turn to. When the singing came to an end—and with no further warning—I heard Dorothy introduce me. The singing had calmed people down, but the emotional intensity remained and many wiped away tears and sniffles. Young innocent people had now had their first experience with police on the rampage.

As I made my way to the pulpit, I recalled the words of God to the prophet Jeremiah, " 'Do not say, "I am only a youth," for to all to whom I send you, you shall go, and whatever I command you, you shall speak. Be not afraid of them, for I am with you to deliver you,' says the Lord. Then the Lord put forth his hand and touched my mouth and the Lord said to me, 'Behold I have put my words in your mouth' " (Jer. 1:7–9, author paraphrase).

By the time I reached the pulpit, I had a clear idea of an approach to this situation that might be helpful to this audience of young people.

"How many people here have ever been chased by a dog before? Raise your hands." Almost every hand was raised.

"How many of you have been hit in the head playing baseball?" Again most hands were raised.

"And how many have ever enjoyed a shower on a hot day?" By this time people began to anticipate my drift. A soft murmur went across the church as I continued.

"When a dog bites you, you get a shot and you heal in a matter of days. If you're hit in the head with a bat, you might get knocked out, but usually, even the knot is gone in a couple of weeks. In a shower on a hot day, like today, your clothes are probably already wet and will dry in a few minutes.

"The issue here is not the dog, the billy clubs, and the fire hoses. We are upset all right, but we are upset about those scars that racism and segregation have put on our psyches and our souls. Those do not heal easily, and they continue to cripple us throughout our lives, just as they have crippled our parents and grandparents.

"The feeling that, 'White is right, if you're yellow you're mellow, if you're brown, stick around, and if you're black, get back' hurts us. This is the sense of inferiority that drives men to drink, that leads girls to get pregnant rather than finish school, that gnaws away at our self-confidence until we begin to believe that we can't do anything right on our own.

"We are marching against an entire system that must be changed. It would do no good to kill the policeman who beats you; he's trapped by the same system. He believes that his white skin makes him superior and that he's supposed to keep you down. Somehow we've got to help even the racist policeman to see that a man can't keep another man down in the gutter unless he keeps one foot down there with him.

"It's time for us to get the entire South out of the ditch. Black and white men and women must rise up together against those things that make us fear and hate each other.

This movement is a movement as Frederick Douglass said, '. . . to save black men's bodies and white men's souls.' "[1]

As the crowd began to "Amen!" and answer back with "Tell the truth!" and "Say it, preacher!" I found myself forgetting my self-consciousness and simply pouring out the feelings in my heart. I don't know how long I talked or what else I said, but the experience of the power of the pulpit, of God actually seeming to put words in my mouth, was a religious experience that moved me to a new level of leadership. This moment was life-changing just as Martin's decision to go to jail and trust in God to "make a way out of no way" raised him to an even higher plane of responsibility.

In that Sunday's paper, an ad sponsored by eight white religious leaders—Protestant, Catholic, and Jewish—castigated Martin for creating racial turmoil in Birmingham.

Martin was furious. There was no writing paper available to him in jail, but Wyatt was allowed to bring *The New York Times* into the jail, and the ideas were stirring so strongly within Martin that he began composing an answer to the white clergy around the margin of the newspaper. All the frustration that had welled up in him through the past disappointing weeks burst forth in an eloquent, passionate, and prophetic answer. When he had exhausted every centimeter of free space in the *Times,* he began to write on toilet tissue, no simple feat with the early generation of ballpoint pens. This was smuggled out and published as "Letter from Birmingham Jail," and it continues to be a source of inspiration even today.

At the time of Martin's arrest in Birmingham, there was no way to anticipate that anything but damage control would come out of it all. For all practical purposes, it seemed to us at the time the movement had failed. However, Easter always follows Good Friday. By Easter Sunday, word of the events surrounding Martin's arrest had spread throughout the city. It was not through the newspaper that people learned what had happened—the newspaper buried the story on page thirty-four. The truth spread by word of mouth through the proverbial grapevine.

On Easter Sunday afternoon we were scheduled to meet at the New Pilgrim Baptist Church. Its pastor, the Reverend Nelson Smith, was in jail with Martin and Ralph Abernathy. Our plan was to meet for a brief mass meeting at 3:00 P.M. and march to the jail a few blocks away to let the prisoners know that we were carrying on the struggle. Marching, singing, and praying seemed to us to be harmless, but again Bull Conner had another idea. He felt good about the performance of his dogs and firemen and was convinced that with the leadership in jail, he could crush the movement with one more show of force. He didn't really understand that a new spirit of confidence and determination was emerging.

We, too, did not understand our opposition. Why should a simple four block walk to the jail, a couple of freedom songs, and a prayer bring out an entire police battalion? We were shocked to see a half dozen bright red fire trucks and the entire canine detail lined across Sixth Avenue blocking our path.

Those marching were not well-trained demonstrators. The people who marched that Easter were a new infusion of talent who had finally awakened to what was happening around them and had decided to stand up and be counted. For most of them, this was their first public resistance to racism and segregation. We had no idea how they would respond to the sight of dogs, police, and a red sea of fire trucks, so we asked everyone to kneel down as we approached the police blockade.

When a group of frightened church people get down

on their knees, they pray. The more fearful they are, the more fervent their prayers. There were over five thousand people in the march on Easter Sunday. It was the largest march ever held in the South at that time. As the mass of marchers prayed, moaned, cried, and began to shout, we attempted to reason with Bull Conner. Our petitions fell on deaf ears.

But our prayers were being heard.

All of a sudden, someone shouted, "God is with this movement; we're going on to the jail." Slowly and deliberately, people began to help each other to their feet, and the march resumed heading right for the dogs and fire trucks. The dogs were no longer barking or straining on their leashes. I distinctly saw a tear in the eye of one of the firemen who was standing there pointing the pressure hose at us. At that close distance, the stream of water would have broken a person's ribs. Bull Conner stood there shouting, "Stop them!" but nobody responded.

The people began singing an old spiritual, "I want Jesus to walk with me. All along my pilgrim journey, Lord, I want Jesus to walk with me." And the marchers passed through the police and fire truck blockade without an incident. When we reached the park across from the jail and once again quieted for prayer, one elderly church sister shouted, "God done parted the Red Sea one mo' time!"

The movement that seemed dead three days earlier now was raised up with new life and enthusiasm. The daily demonstrations built until there was no more room in the jails. Whole student populations began to walk out of their school buildings and march downtown singing, ready to go to jail for freedom. High school students were organized and given some nonviolent training by James Bevel, James Orange, and the Rev. C. T. Vivian who had joined us from Nashville. The training included daily Bible study and group discussions on how to make use of their newfound freedom. The students knew they must remain nonviolent and polite even to their jailers. Jail became a school of faith and freedom, much like the jailings of Paul and Silas in the New Testament. The older people who had begun the demonstrations and had been in jail for several weeks began to teach and share their faith and wisdom with these new converts to the freedom struggle.

Through all of the demonstrations, I had been in contact with the Birmingham business leadership. We met several afternoons a week at Carpenter House, the Episcopal Diocesan Headquarters. This was done through Peggy Horne and the Episcopal Bishop George M. Murray, one of the signers of the clergy letter to Martin, who had responded positively to the impassioned appeal of Martin's letter from the jail.

In a few more weeks, everyone was out of jail. We had negotiated a schedule for desegregating public accommodations, a plan for hiring black clerks and managers, and a commitment to encourage voter registration and school desegregation. The agreement was made with a committee of one hundred Birmingham business leaders and was supported by the national efforts of Burke Marshall of the U.S. Justice Department and the National Business Roundtable. America was mobilized morally, and once again, when there was no way to bring about such massive and dramatic changes, God made a way out of no way.

The action in Birmingham sparked the conscience of the nation. It also sparked similar protests as far away as South Africa. The global human rights movement was born in Birmingham, and the leadership that strove to "redeem the soul of America" began to see it would also help to change the world. Confidence began to soar. It worked. Nonviolent, direct action was a force more powerful than a nuclear bomb. With it we could help change the world without destroying either person or property.

New leadership was developing. Weak, inadequate, and imperfect as we were, we were learning that the power of God could empower each of us, even me, and that the grace of God was able to transform a country that had been racially divided for centuries. In 1963 we could imagine a civil rights bill from Washington that would change the legal framework of the South, but we could not even dream that one day the Berlin Wall would come down with citizens of East and West Germany singing together, "We shall overcome."

8

Bless Those That Persecute You

When Martin Luther King, Jr.'s home was bombed in Montgomery back in 1956, the men of the neighborhood came to the scene of the bombing carrying weapons. This was a natural response. Everyone in the nation had been conditioned by the violence of World War II. Most of the men were veterans of that war and beneficiaries of extensive military training.

But Martin, even as a young man of twenty-six, had a vision of another possible approach to the problems and conflicts we faced as human beings. He urged the men to go home and take their guns back to the safety of their closets. "If we follow the Old Testament law of 'An eye for an eye and a tooth for a tooth,' we will just end up with a nation that is blind and toothless. No," he said, "we must discover 'a more excellent way.'"

Martin was using the terminology of the apostle Paul in his letter to the Corinthians as he introduced the beautiful psalm of love in 1 Corinthians 13. Martin was also strongly influenced by the nonviolent ideas of Mahatma Gandhi in his successful drive for India's independence.

Gandhi challenged India to resist evil without resorting to evil. He accepted the spiritual potential of India as worthy of cultivation. "Love of the hater is the most difficult of all. But by the grace of God, even this most difficult thing becomes easy to accomplish if we want to do it."[1]

In our struggles against southern racism, we too chose to accept this moral and pragmatic challenge. We understood that it would not help us to get an education if we destroyed schools, nor would it help us to get jobs if we destroyed factories. Our intent was to be included in the life of America, and this required a moral struggle. We were trying to create brothers, not enemies, so like Gandhi we began to engage in experiments with the truth and power of nonviolence.

When Martin went to jail in Albany, Georgia in 1962, I was a new arrival in the movement. I was given the task of visiting him in jail twice daily to keep him informed of the movement's progress and problems. On my first visit, I entered the jail and said politely, "Excuse me, I'd like to see Dr. King, please." Without even looking up, the desk sergeant shouted to the jailer, "There's a little nigger out here to see those big niggers back there."

I was so taken aback that I didn't know what to do. To express my indignation would only get me thrown in jail or barred from visiting, and someone had to be able to move in and out of the jail to keep information flowing if it were at all possible. Violence was no answer. The sergeant was a six-foot five-inch, 250-pound, former football player with a stick and a gun. I did, however, make note of his name on his uniform. When I came back the next day, I addressed him by name. "Good morning, Sergeant Hamilton, how are you doing today?"

Now, he seemed shocked, and grunted, "Okay."

From that time on, I never went to the jail without addressing Sergeant Hamilton by name and engaging him in some brief small talk before asking to see Dr. King. He never again spoke disrespectfully to me, and we actually became familiar with each other's families and sports interests. Of course, as everyone in the southern farm belt does, we talked about the weather. I not only survived, I accomplished my mission and visited the jail daily until Martin was released.

Constant confrontation with people with whom you differ requires some solution. Most of the time, black people just avoided the confrontation and accepted the mutual animosity. That was the pattern of behavior before the movement. But for black Americans it was impossible to completely avoid confrontation and humiliation. These problems almost always occurred when we were least prepared and least expected it.

Through the civil rights movement we attempted to change the pattern of avoidance and accidental confrontation which left so many black people intimidated, demeaned, and insecure. Our movement was to change the relationship from one of fear and distrust to a relationship of respect and understanding. That meant we had to aggressively challenge the system and its violence. We chose to confront the system, not with violence, but with aggressive, organized, disciplined goodwill.

For years we had read the Sermon on the Mount in the gospel of Matthew:

> Love your enemies, bless those who curse you, do good to those who hate you, and pray for those who spitefully use you and persecute you, that you may be sons of your Father in heaven; for He makes His sun rise on the evil and on the good, and sends rain on the just and on the unjust.
>
> (Matt. 5:44–45)

Now, with nonviolent direct action, we had a method with which to bring alive that radical notion that all men, women, and children belonged to the same heavenly Father. We pursued this method as the means by which we could make Christ's call at least a partial reality and not just a utopian ideal.

Nonviolent direct action seeks to change an unjust situation by addressing it openly and publicly in an attempt to raise it "before the court of world opinion"[2] in the confidence that it can be changed without violence. There is no guarantee, of course, and no method is foolproof. However, with nonviolence or, as Gandhi called it, "truth force," neither person nor property is destroyed. At times you will be called on to suffer, but never will you inflict suffering.

There is a strange power in innocent suffering. We see it in the book of Acts with the conversion of the apostle Paul as he is moved to reorient his life after viewing the martyrdom of Stephen. I have never been one to seek suffering, and I believe that God must lead one onto the path of suffering. A person's ambition or need for attention will not suffice in the face of suffering. However, one day my number came up in St. Augustine, Florida in the summer of 1964.

St. Augustine was a tough place. Hosea Williams, a chemist with the U.S. Department of Agriculture, had recently joined our SCLC staff, and he had gone to St. Augustine to work with the movement.

Hosea was a disabled veteran of World War II who had been in a foxhole in Germany and suffered a direct hit by a Nazi bomb. Everyone in the foxhole was killed except Hosea. He survived and, after a year in veterans' hospitals, returned to Georgia where he was roughed up by local police in a Greyhound Bus station for drinking water from the only working fountain on a hot summer day. Of course, in 1945 even a disabled veteran of the war was still a second-class citizen. Hosea's passion for justice was fired by this incident, and he became convinced that God had saved him in Germany so that he could fight for justice in the United States. This made him an extremely valuable member of Dr. King's team, but one who was always too ready to demonstrate.

In the summer of 1964, the Civil Rights Act was being debated in the Congress, and further demonstrations seemed unnecessary. The SCLC strategy called for a careful marshaling of our limited resources and a deliberate selection of our points of confrontation. The national situation was moving along fairly well in the Congress. The Interreligious Council on Religion and Race had mobilized national religious bodies to support the Civil Rights Bill, and it seemed just a matter of time until the bill passed. How long could the traditional filibuster last? St. Augustine didn't seem to be necessary to our plan of action, so Martin sent me down there to "wind the movement down gracefully" and bring Hosea home.

I arrived in St. Augustine in the late evening. There was a white mob gathered around the town square. I went directly to the church to join the mass meeting in progress. About one hundred people, mostly older women and young teenagers, were gathered in a small church. As Hosea saw me enter at the back of the church, he announced, "Reverend Andy Young is here to lead the demonstration," and he called for volunteers to march with me down to the Old Slave Market near the town square.

At that point, I had no intention of leading anyone into that mob. They were shouting and drinking and generally trying to intimidate anyone who might want to challenge the traditions represented by the Old Slave Market. But I didn't want anyone else to lead people down there either.

When I discovered that this march had already been announced, and any cancellation would appear to be cowardice, I decided that I would lead the march in order to keep things under control. There had been little or no training in St. Augustine, and that mob was as mean a crowd as I had ever seen.

We marched from the church with just about thirty demonstrators. It was not a very impressive group after the thousands that had marched in Birmingham. But then movements always seemed to start with only the chosen, courageous few. I was trying to decide just how far we could go and yet avoid a confrontation. But what I didn't consider was that these were people who were standing up against segregation for the first time in their lives. It was not just another march for them. It was their first march toward freedom, and they could not turn back. They had been singing, "Oh freedom, Oh freedom over me, and before I'll be a slave, I'd be buried in my grave, and go home to my Lord and be free."

As we approached the street leading to the town square, we were stopped by Sheriff L. O. Davis. He told us to turn around and go back. There was a mob of four or five hundred people in the square, and he only had twenty-seven men on his force, so they could not possibly assure us of safety or offer any protection against that mob. He had already convinced me, but I asked the group to form a circle so that we could pray for guidance.

My prayer was an honest, simple appeal for guidance. I didn't ask God to protect us because I was ready to go back to the church. As far as I was concerned, the risks were too great for a handful of women and children. A march of thirty men would have been much less risky. These mobs seldom, if ever, attacked a group of men, but black men rarely had the courage to lead demonstrations. They had much more to lose.

Typically, individual black men were the primary victims of intimidation, job loss, violence, or even loss of their lives. So, many black men hid behind the macho pose that they couldn't be nonviolent. Occasionally I would shame them by charging, "You and your family are oppressed every day, and you've never been violent to anybody white!" The men were nonviolent daily when confronted by white people. I would go on, "We don't count stabbing your buddies in a crap game or beating your wife and children. That's not being violent, that's being sick. You take your frustrations out on the people who love you rather than confront the people who are daily denying you your freedom, your education, your job security, and your advancement just because of the color of your skin."

It was always frustrating that we couldn't get more men, especially young men, to participate. Usually young male SCLC staff members who had been brought in as part of the training team marched with the local people, and they were often the only men in the march.

And tonight was no different; we still lacked men. But much to my surprise, we had a cadre of determined, nonviolent warriors, even though they were mostly women and teenagers.

After I prayed, one of the "good ol' sisters" sang out in a loud, clear voice: "Be not dismayed, whate'er betide, God will take care of you. Beneath his wings of love abide, God will take care of you."

Then everyone joined in on the chorus: "God will take care of you, through every day . . . all the way; He will take care of you, God will take care of you."

We sang out an affirmation of faith that was about to be tested. I finally realized that there was no turning back for any logical or pragmatic reason. So I was trapped, but I was still determined that we could finish this march without anyone being hurt.

We marched, still singing softly, "God will take care of you." And I thought to myself, *It's one thing to sing this in church where it's easy to believe it, but the song says through every day, and this is nighttime in St. Augustine.* The mob was still a block away, but they, too, became strangely quiet when they realized that we were marching toward them. The silence was broken by the rattle of chains and the shattering of a bottle. It was easy to anticipate what they had in mind. Mobs could do almost anything under the cover of night, especially when they really had the support of the local law enforcement.

I began to understand what it meant to "walk through the valley of the shadow of death . . . [and] fear no evil" (Ps. 23:4 KJV). I was not afraid for some reason, perhaps because I was determined that none of those good people get hurt.

I remember being very disturbed when one of the ministers walking with me heard the shattering of glass and murmured an expletive. I simply said, "Don't cuss—pray."

Soon, we approached a road blocked by a group of burly white men. I stopped the march and decided that I must try to talk with them. There was no turning back, so I walked over to the gang. I later learned the gang was led by "Hoss" Manucy, an underprivileged white man who really thought that his security and survival depended on keeping blacks down. Hoss was seen on national television bragging, "I'm a good Christian. I don't smoke; I don't drink; I just beat niggers."

The sheriff was nowhere to be found. I don't think I even got a word out. I was standing there face-to-face with the one man who seemed like the leader, and then someone blindsided me. I didn't feel a thing, but I remember being hit in the jaw with someone's best punch and almost simultaneously being clubbed with what must have been a blackjack. From then on, it was lights out. Only several years later did I see a film clip of the beating I took. I was stomped and kicked and probably only spared serious injury because I instinctively rolled into a ball and protected my head and stomach from direct blows.

When I came to my senses, I was being helped to my feet by Willie Bolden of the SCLC staff, who had come to my rescue. I didn't feel any physical pain or fear. I was only determined that we keep on marching. All of our thinking and training had taught us that if you let violence deter you, you're only empowering and encouraging violence. At this point, even though I was probably not aware of what I was doing or what had happened to me, I knew that we could not let this violence stop our march. If it did, it would soon crush our movement.

Martin was fond of preaching, "We will match your ability to inflict suffering with our ability to endure suffering in the confidence that unearned suffering is redemptive."

The mob had left me on the ground and moved back into the park, certain that I had learned my lesson. As I came back to the front of the line I said, "We can't stop now, let's go." And slowly but surely the straggling band of nonviolent marchers continued. I then remember someone in the mob cussing and saying, "Them niggers got some nerve."

I don't know what motivated us to march on, but it certainly wasn't cheekiness. It was closer to faith and determined belief that "the Lord will make a way out of no way." But the way was not to open yet. The same gang moved to the entry of the park closest to the Old Slave Market and once again blocked our way. Again I kept marching slowly and surely until they stood a few feet in front of us.

This time, I did get to utter a couple of sentences. "We are not here to do you any harm," I said simply. "We merely want to have a word of prayer at this place where our ancestors were bought and sold as slaves, to ask God to help us end slavery in all its forms."

Just as I finished my sentence, a young boy burst through the crowd and attempted to kick me in my testicles. Fortunately this time I saw him coming and shifted just a bit to the side. As I bent over to avoid the kick, the blackjack again came across my head. This time it merely hurt and left a knot. I did not go down and, thank God, I did not go out. (For months later, I kept wishing I could meet one of these guys alone and away from St. Augustine and the discipline of the movement. I was still struggling with a total commitment to nonviolence, but I had no question that it was the only tactic that had a chance for success in the South.)

Then, as if by magic, Sheriff Davis appeared and waved the crowd away with one sweep of his hand and said, "Let 'em through." And we walked on to the Old Slave Market, knelt in prayer, and then returned to the church without incident.

After it was over, I felt a real sense of triumph. No one was seriously hurt. My bruises lasted for months but a new sense of personal confidence also became a part of my life. This had been a real test, and I hadn't faltered.

We demonstrated at the beaches and swimming pools during the day. The marches continued at night. The federal court, under Judge Brian Simpson, ordered the sheriff to protect us. Judge Simpson also exposed the connection among the Klan, the mob, the Ancient City Gun Club, and the Office of Sheriff's Deputies. They were one and the same.

As the movement progressed, St. Augustine may have become our bloodiest struggle. In subsequent demonstrations, we were not able to limit the attacks to a single person; almost everyone suffered in St. Augustine. But I have never seen a more determined people. They went to jail or to the hospitals, and when they were released, they were back in the demonstrations.

In St. Augustine my wife joined in a march for the first time where I was working. Jean often demonstrated in Atlanta, and I tried my best to convince her that *her* movement was teaching children—our own three daughters and those with whom she worked in the Atlanta public school system. I argued her task was helping the young to be ready to contribute in an integrated society. She insisted on joining me in St. Augustine. I did not march in the same demonstration with Jean. It was our policy that loved ones not be allowed to take part in the same demonstrations. It put too much strain on one's commitment to nonviolence. It is much easier to suffer yourself than it is to stand by and watch your wife or children be attacked.

The experience of marching through the hate-filled mob was frightening. With faces contorted and venomous language flowing from their mouths, the people in the mob waved iron pipes and clenched fists.

But Jean says she will always remember the words of the elderly black woman with whom she marched: "Ain't they sad?"

On July 2, 1964, President Lyndon Johnson signed the historic civil rights package. Martin went to join Roy Wilkins of the NAACP, Whitney Young of the Urban League, and others for the signing of this bill into law, which committed the United States of America to the enforcement of protection for the rights of all citizens. This legislation also included protection for the rights of women and Hispanic citizens who, though they did not share the legacy of slavery, still experienced wide discrimination.

Hosea Williams and I remained around St. Augustine. We decided to celebrate July fourth with friends and family and give people a chance to discuss the Civil Rights Bill and its meaning in St. Augustine. Our plan was to test the enforcement and implementation of desegregated public accommodations after the holiday.

After several weeks of having walked "through the valley of the shadow of death," we were pleasantly surprised by the friendly but nervous reception we received as we went to the very places where we previously had been brutalized and arrested and quietly ordered coffee. When the nervous waitress poured coffee to overflowing and offered apologetically to get a new cup, I was filled with joy as I thought: *Thou preparest a table before me in the presence of mine enemies: thou annointest my head with oil; my [coffee] cup runneth over.*

The refusal to hate, the willingness to forgive and begin a new pattern of relationships under federally enforced law marked a new era for the South and the nation. Southern white churches had not been in the forefront of the struggle for racial justice, but once the law changed, they encouraged and supported compliance. The resistance melted surprisingly fast. We experienced one of the most radical shifts in law and tradition in human history. It was accomplished with very little violence and suffering, when compared with the armed conflict and terrorism which characterizes most movements for social change.

The American South almost immediately began to heal its wounds and begin an era in which it would inspire and provide leadership for the nation and the world. The emergence of men and women of talent and vision from the South led to the election of several of the nation's most progressive and innovative governors. One of them,

Jimmy Carter, became president in 1976 and made the American ideal—"that all men [and women and children] are created equal, and endowed with certain unalienable rights"—an important element of America's foreign policy. Over time I moved from a battered form lying in the streets of St. Augustine to the halls of the United Nations as ambassador and spokesman for our nation's human rights policy.

This degree of rapid progress and prosperity was possible only because in our struggle we destroyed no resources. We overcame evil with love and discovered that there is a power of the Spirit that can change people and nations more effectively than bombs and bullets.

I will always cherish two memories of St. Augustine that symbolize nonviolence at its best. First, that a small group of women and young people had the faith that "God will take care of you." This unwavering belief led them out into that night of hatred and violence with a quiet courage and determination. And second, the beautiful sound of the black community singing as the Ku Klux Klan marched through St. Augustine on a Saturday evening, after having inflicted their hatred and violence on us for weeks.

As the Klan passed by, black people greeted them singing, "I love everybody in my heart."

9

The Spirit Is A'movin' All Over the Land

From the passage of the Civil Rights Act of 1964, things seemed to move rapidly forward. Martin received the Nobel Prize for Peace later that year, and the movement reached a new level of success and respect. Nonviolent social change was working.

Young people began to question the wisdom of war anywhere in the world, and movements for change began among women, Mexican American farm workers, American Indians, and white Appalachian workers in the fields of Kentucky and the coal mines of West Virginia. Consumers and students concerned about the protection of our natural environment began to scrutinize the practices of both government and multi-national corporations.

Things seemed to be progressing in a reasonable and positive manner. Suddenly, just a few weeks after President Johnson signed the Voting Rights Act of 1965 into law, the fires of Watts exploded in Los Angeles. This was a dark period indeed. We had just begun to break down walls of race and class in the South, but now the rest of the nation was erupting.

In 1965, with the success of the movement at its peak, SCLC was still a group of one hundred and fifty staff nationwide with an annual budget of less than a million dollars. Despite our limitations it seemed the nation expected us to solve the problems produced by four hundred years of slavery and racial segregation. It was too much and we were too few, but we poured our very lives into accepting this challenge.

The next few years were both the most exciting and the most frustrating of my life. After focusing on racism alone, the movement now began to address the problems of poverty through our Poor People's Campaign of 1968. This added a dimension that was for our opponents the straw that broke the camel's back. Race problems in the South and the war in Vietnam had strained the nation's capacity to grow and understand. Political and religious leaders who had been very strong and clear on the moral dimensions of racial segregation were unable to agree with Martin's ideas that the bombs we dropped on Vietnam were exploding at home in unemployment and inflation.

There was no real public argument made against us; however, our patriotism was questioned. God's people always find it difficult to comprehend change when it goes against the idols of the nation. In the late 1960s, the military containment of what we saw as a communist threat was our leading national idolatry.

Our questioning of the national priority of death and destruction with a call to life and development of the nation's poor through a poor people's march was too much. The forces of evil conspired to take from us a mighty son of God who had hoped to help us make this world more like the kingdom of God. On April 4, 1968, in the cool of a beautiful spring evening, as the azaleas and dogwoods blessed the greenery with color, Martin Luther King, Jr. was shot.

This was the end. Martin was lying in his own blood on the balcony of the Lorraine Motel in Memphis, Tennessee. He looked so peaceful and angelic. He probably never even heard the shot. He had been laughing and joking a few minutes earlier as though he didn't have a care in the world.

We were on the way out to dinner when I heard the sound. *Some jerk is playing with firecrackers,* I thought. Then I looked to the balcony and saw no Martin. My first thought was, *He's clowning again. He probably went back into the room with Ralph.* Then I saw his shoe sticking through the iron railing. His foot was no longer in it. I rushed up the stairs and there he was. At peace, maybe for the first time in his young thirty-nine years.

I almost envied him. "Soon I will be done with the troubles of the world," the spiritual says, and that is an affirmation of faith and a proclamation of hope. In our tradition, death meant "going home" to live with God. In our tradition, death was a blessing to be welcomed, not an end to be feared.

But that was the end for Martin, and God knows he had earned his rest. He had borne the trials and tribulations of a nation bent on destroying itself with violence over racial differences. He had taught that it was possible to live together without violence. He had anguished over our failures and blindness to the ultimate reality of our brotherhood and sisterhood as we nitpicked over differences of color and opportunity. And the dream of justice and equal opportunity planted in his heart from the inspiration of the prophets prevailed over all doubt and cynicism. He was a believer, and he helped those around him to believe. Now, just as we were beginning to get a movement together, he was gone.

We all believed there was no way we could do anything now. We would continue because we must, but there was little hope that we could have any impact on the world without Martin.

Without Martin the combination of moral authority, tactical wisdom, intellectual perspective, and mass appeal did not reside in any one civil rights leader. Martin Luther King, Jr. stood alone in that category. It seemed everyone in the movement asked, "What will we do, now that the King of love is dead?" Because when Martin Luther King, Jr. died on April 4, 1968, all the hope and trust which he inspired seemed to die with him.

With Martin gone, there was no longer one clear voice, no clarion vision to hold the civil rights movement together and give the people a sense of direction. Several protest candidates emerged. All of my good friends seemed incapable of adjusting to the new realities. Alienation reached new levels in the liberal community and among intellectuals, and bitterness and confusion prevailed. Still, for the most part, poor people knew that the work we had done in the 1960s had made a difference, and "the spirit was a'movin' all over the land." Only we who were closest to Martin could not see right away what was happening.

There was little hope for real change to come through the Poor People's Campaign. At best, we hoped to call the nation's attention to the poverty throughout America so that the next president would have mandate for positive social change. Of course, we were thinking that the next president would be Robert Kennedy or at least Hubert Humphrey.

I'm afraid that we in the movement were all a little too naive. We really believed in the federal government, the FBI, and even the Congress, though we knew it to be dominated by people whose very election depended on keeping us out of the system. We knew the ambiguities in the minds and politics of both Kennedy and Johnson, but we remained confident that in America we could create the moral conditions wherein political leaders could and would "do the right thing." We never considered that their hearts were not with us, for we were certain that we were moving in the direction of the Kingdom of God.

Certainly obstacles to the movement were there, but often they were from forces we could not see. I always saw Martin's death as a political assassination. His death coincided closely in time with those of President John Kennedy, Senator Robert Kennedy, and Malcolm X—all people close to the movement. And there were other deaths: Robert Spike of the Commission on Religion and Race was mysteriously murdered at Ohio State University; Stephen Courier, whose family coordinated much of the private foundation financial support of the movement, especially the Voter Education Project and the bail bonds for our Birmingham demonstrators, disappeared in the infamous Bermuda Triangle; Walter Reuther of the United Auto Workers died in a plane crash.

Each of these untimely deaths was treated as an isolated incident, and there is a plausible explanation for each. All those who died also happened to be friends of mine, and all happened to be extremely important in building a coalition of conscience to facilitate nonviolent social change. These deaths might well have been unrelated incidents, but this was a period in our nation's life when the politics of assassination were an accepted part of our nation's foreign policy. It would be naive to assume that those sinister influences did not also have a domestic impact.

Dick Gregory, in his profoundly humorous approach to life, was fond of saying, "If you're black in America and not slightly paranoid, you're really sick." Certainly a healthy realism about our politics and government bureaucracy was essential for emotional and political survival. Martin always reminded us that we never knew "the day nor the hour" when, as with the rich young ruler, the Lord will say, "This day is thy soul required of thee."

But one must never be deterred or distracted by fear or conspiracy theories. There is some truth in all of them, but there is no virtue in documenting and proving beyond a shadow of a doubt the sin and insecurity of people and their institutions. This is a given. We would not need movements in the first place if individuals and systems were generous and fair. It is because they are not that they must be challenged, that they will be challenged.

Our early goal had been to make that challenge as non-violent and spiritually true as is humanly possible. For we, too, "like sheep have gone astray" (Isa. 53:6 KJV). All men sin and fall short of the glory of God, and women do too.

We need a democracy with enough freedom to challenge the inequities generated by sin wherever and however it manifests itself. That's why a free press is important, even when it's wrong, sensationalist, and excessive. The media raise doubts and questions of justice and integrity on a daily basis. And if they are only right once a week, they justify their existence, especially if the accused can also have access to the same free press to answer the charges and accusations.

There can be no democracy without truth. There can be no truth without controversy, and there can be no change without freedom. And without freedom, there can be no progress. This is the irony of the so-called progressive governments that have remained stagnant and have never progressed. It is also true of the big businesses that managed away their profits in an attempt to control their personnel and market share rather than freely compete.

The assassination of so many political and social leaders in the 1960s who were critical of America's vision of itself

probably set back the cause of freedom at least twenty
years. The Nixon administration institutionalized these
setbacks through the appointment of conservative judges,
the shift of expenditures to the defense industry, and, perhaps worst of all, by abandoning America's leadership role
in the world economy by repudiating the post-war Bretton Woods Agreements. Let me digress a moment and
look at the Bretton Woods Agreements more closely—an
agreement which had provided economic stability for the
post-war world for twenty-five years.

Bretton Woods had provided a stable currency for the
world which was pegged to the dollar, reasonable interest
rates that encouraged development through public and
private investment, and free access to technology and mar-
kets. From 1945 to 1973, the world grew and prospered
under cooperative American leadership, which led with a
strong dollar backed by gold.

One of my first congressional hearings was as a member
of the Banking Sub-committee on International Finance,
where in 1973 the Nixon Administration appeared *en
masse* to advocate the end of U.S.-backed stability for the
world monetary system. No one knew quite why. The
arguments seemed based more on economic theories than
practical evidence.

But George Schultz, Secretary of the Treasury, Paul
Volker, then Assistant Secretary for International Monetary Affairs, and Arthur Burns, Chairman of the Federal
Reserve Bank all said that they agreed on this course of
action or, really, inaction. Twenty years later, Paul Volker,
in his book *Changing Fortunes,* admitted that all of these
distinguished men had grave reservations about their rec-
ommendation at the time, but they were going along with
the new administration's position. I questioned them, and
as the lowest-ranking member of the Committee, admit-
tedly did not understand the meaning and implications of

their actions. But without some strong agreement and leadership, it seemed that politics would increasingly influence currencies and prices.

Less than six months after this decision was taken, the Organization of Petroleum Exporting Countries (OPEC) was formed, the price of oil went from $3.50 per barrel to eventual highs of $50.00, and a major shift in our nation's economic fortunes began. One of the greatest shifts in wealth in the history of the planet was about to occur, and the global economy went from a situation of gradual stable growth for twenty-five years under U.S. leadership, vision, and sacrifice, to the current economic roller coaster which had led to worldwide anxiety, economic stagnation, and joblessness.

This matter has never received sufficient attention and discussion. The press and the Congress got caught up in the Watergate scandal, and thanks again to the spirit moving across the South, southern Democrats were freed to vote their conscience, confident of their new protection from black voters in the coming elections.

Nixon was maligned and forced to resign because of the Watergate break-in scandal. But the greatest damage he did to the nation and to the world and his greatest crime may have been the abdication of American global leadership and financial vision. Whenever I think about this I mourn again the assassinations of Martin Luther King, Jr. and Robert Kennedy, and I lament Hubert Humphrey's loss in 1968 by less than 1 percent of the vote. Things might have been so different.

Forgive the digression, but even thoughts must be allowed to flow freely and uncensored when the "spirit is a'movin' all over the land."

That's why we had to keep moving in the months immediately following Martin's death. It was of the utmost importance that the dream live on. "I ain't got time to die," the spiritual reminds us. We could not afford to get sidetracked, even to pursue and convict the killers and conspirators. Our mission was to bring justice to the least of God's children and to feed the hungry, clothe the naked, and heal the sick.

Soon the election of Richard Nixon seemed to threaten that possibility. The political agenda Nixon represented was an active attempt to reverse government assistance to the poor; it attempted to divide and conquer America by playing up fears regarding bussing of school children, welfare fraud, and the abdication of states' rights. To us, these were just sophisticated ways of saying, "Stop the niggers —they are going too far, too fast." This was, to us, quite a betrayal of the party best represented by Abraham Lincoln.

But people who had never stopped to listen to Martin when he was alive suddenly became aware of the powerful truth of his message. Civil rights legislation had been passed in 1964 and in 1965, but little had been done to enforce or implement many of the guidelines. Now the cumbersome bureaucratic machinery of the federal government and of the Fortune 500 companies began to creep into motion.

American colleges and universities realized that the Kerner Commission report on urban violence was an indictment of the entire society, and they too began to make an effort to heal the wounds of racism through broadening their curriculum and recruiting black students and teachers. More African American students entered major academic institutions than at any previous time in our history. The nation's mainstream decided that the American dream articulated so eloquently by Martin at the March on Washington in 1963 was rapidly turning into a nightmare that jeopardized the future of us all.

Quietly, a few individuals were moved to heroic acts. Maynard Jackson, a young African American attorney in

Atlanta, decided to challenge Senator Herman Talmadge for the United States Senate from Georgia. Nobody thought that Jackson could win, but people needed to express their indignation, support, and yes, rage at the ballot box. Maynard did lose that race, but went on to become Atlanta's first African American vice mayor in 1969 and mayor in 1973.

Even in the civil rights movement days when Martin was alive, we knew that ultimately politics would effect changes we needed. The Sunday before he went to Memphis, Martin had held a brief meeting in New York to discuss how we might begin to transfer some of the enormous energy that we had generated in the streets for demonstrations into politics. He had invited Harry Belafonte, Congressman John Conyers of Michigan, Mayor Richard Hatcher of Gary, Indiana, and me to begin thinking about the political nature of our civil rights efforts with a special emphasis on electing men and women of goodwill. After all, we reasoned, we shouldn't have to march for every problem. We should be able to elect people of sensitivity and accountability to represent us and address our needs. What Martin called the "coalition of conscience" had to make a place in American politics.

I saw my role as that of a facilitator. I planned to help elect people to government using some of the organizing skills I had acquired in the movement. I had also learned a bit about fundraising that I thought would prove helpful. (Years later, I was able to use all our movement experience to enter electoral politics.)

Now the Fifth Congressional District of Georgia seemed like a good place to field a candidate for 1970. Atlanta had a reputation as a progressive city, and the African American population was almost 40 percent of the total vote. It was my belief that the race could be won by Julian Bond, an articulate young graduate of the Student

Nonviolent Coordinating Committee (SNCC) who was then serving in the Georgia Legislature.

John Lewis, then chairman of the Southwide Voter Education Project and former chairman of SNCC, wrote a beautiful letter to Julian, describing what he thought it would take for him to win such a race. After a meeting of the Board of the Southern Christian Leadership Conference on which John and I both served, we decided to phone Julian and convince him to run.

Julian responded very clearly to our request. His family had met and decided that he should not run. I always suspected that it was a family decision more than a personal decision, but I respected his family loyalty and his political decisiveness.

John's letter suggested that we needed a candidate who was not afraid to campaign aggressively among white voters, a candidate who could raise money nationwide and who could attract large numbers of young people as volunteers. After Julian declined, John turned to me and said, "You should run. You can fill all those criteria." I laughed and said, "Let me think about it and talk to Jean." Then I headed for the airport and a meeting in New York with Harry Belafonte.

When I arrived at Harry's office, I shared John's letter with him and related our conversation. I still had not been home to discuss it with Jean and my three daughters. But Harry ignored my musings and picked up the phone to call his wife, Julie. I was sure it was some urgent family business that I had interrupted, but Harry simply said, "Check my schedule, and check with Sidney [Poitier], Lena [Horne], and Alan [King]. Let's see if we can find a date for a benefit. Andy's going to run for Congress."

I had not had an opportunity to discuss this with Jean nor had I gone through my usual anguish over the decision. This one seemed right. I was on my way to Congress. It took two tries. I lost in 1970, but learned a lot about myself, the district, and campaigning.

My election to Congress in 1972 made me the first African American member of the United States Congress from the deep South since Reconstruction and the first from Georgia since Jefferson Franklin Long 101 years before. That in itself made me something of a celebrity, a status that I enjoyed but didn't really take seriously. There was a moral authority attached to Martin, SCLC, and those of us who were a part of the southern civil rights movement. That was what made people stop and listen when it was my turn to speak in the Banking Committee or on the floor of the House of Representatives. Yes, I was speaking for the citizens of the Fifth Congressional District of Georgia, a district that was still a majority white district, but I was mandated by the spirit of the movement which still was "a'movin' all over the land."

Barbara Jordan was elected from Houston, Texas and Yvonne Braithwaite Burke from Los Angeles as the other new black members of the Ninety-third Congress. We joined a well-established Congressional Black Caucus which, when spread throughout the committee structure of Congress, exercised a considerable amount of influence in the House, even during the Nixon administration.

In spite of the election of Richard Nixon, the new Congress began to make an impact on the nation's politics. The new members were heavily influenced by the activism of the times and came to Congress imbued with the spirit of change. Within the first term, we were able to develop a consensus to reform the seniority system of the House of Representatives, introduce legislation to create a Congressional Budget Office, stop the bombing of Vietnam, and begin hearings in the Judiciary Committee that led to the resignation of Vice President Agnew and then President Nixon. Gerald Ford then became president.

I found the Congress an exciting place to continue my ministry. The camaraderie and commitment of the members was as wholesome and dedicated as that of my associates in the movement. Though there was not the constant risk of death, and there was considerably more in the way of rewards, the political life with its criticism, scrutiny, and pressure from various constituencies was not without its risks.

Democracy, to be effective, requires that leaders perform heroically. John Kennedy understood this and illustrated it in his book, *Profiles in Courage*. The emergence of southern governors like Jimmy Carter in Georgia, Reuben Askew in Florida, and Dale Bumpers in Arkansas offered a new spirit of fairness and equity which began to produce a new South.

It has been difficult to fulfill the hopes and dreams that grew out of the movement. In retrospect we should not have expected complete fulfillment. It is not and never has been the work and planning of men and women that produces the elements of grace and peace which move life forward. It has always been the love of God, making a way where there is no way. Not until we have given our all and opened ourselves to that power within and beyond that inspires the hearts of men and women to do the impossible, even the unthinkable, do we see signs of the kingdom here on earth.

The struggle continues. "For we do not wrestle against flesh and blood, but against principalities, against powers, against the rulers of the darkness of this age, against spiritual hosts of wickedness in the heavenly places" (Eph. 6:12).

Celebrating the movement of the spirit always leads one to new challenges. The threat of nuclear destruction and the Cold War seem to be behind us. We have seen Polish workers confront armed communist forces with their voices raised in song. I have been privileged to share in the reunification and reconstruction of Germany and have seen pastors and students inspired by a nonviolent legacy assume leadership and begin the unification of all Europe. The world was thrilled at the sight of Nelson Mandela's triumphant exit from twenty-seven years of imprisonment and the image of a lone Chinese youth standing bravely for freedom in front of a tank in Beijing.

All of these courageous acts are testimony to the power of the spirit of nonviolence moving across the planet. That is why the work of Martin's widow, Coretta Scott King, and his sister, Christine, in founding the Martin Luther King, Jr. Center for Nonviolent Social Change is so important. No one else is training people in the theory and practice of nonviolence, and violence is still running rampant across the planet. Even as I write this, we are faced with the ethnic violence and bloodshed in the former Yugoslavia between Serbs, Croatians, and the Muslims of Bosnia, and the ugly reemergence of neo-Nazi activity in Germany. The horror of chaos and famine plagues the Sudan and Somalia. War and greed ravage Liberia and Angola while Zaire seems to just rot away. A Nigerian pastor proclaims that "God must punish Lagos, or He will have to apologize to Sodom and Gomorrah." Though surely there are ten good men in Lagos, if only in his own distinguished family.

The message is that even as we solve one problem or two, there is an abundance of evil loose in the world that yet awaits us.

One recent evening as I knelt in prayer beside the bed of my six-year-old granddaughter, Taylor Marie, I was tempted to pray that God would strengthen me to make the world a better place so she might grow in peace and prosperity. Indeed the world is better than it was forty years ago as we began my generation's struggles.

But I do not pray for God to protect Taylor and Kemet and Lena, our other grandchildren, from the struggle that has so powerfully helped me to know God and the presence of his Spirit at work in the world. Rather our prayer for our grandchildren and our children is that they come to know the presence and the power of God in the midst of the turmoil and challenge of their lives. And that they continue the struggle against the evils and injustices of their time, whatever and wherever they may be.

10

Lead Kindly Light

It's easy to believe in miracles in the Georgia spring-time. The dogwoods enliven the newly green forest and all around the azaleas shout forth the colorful message that the earth has again awakened. Birds long lost to most urban areas still chirp away in the wooded Atlanta landscape, and every now and then the rat-a-tat-tat of a red-crested woodpecker or the frantic squalls of flirtatious blue jays warn that nature is now moving full speed ahead.

On just such a wonderful spring day in 1974, a drama began that would eventually lead Jimmy Carter to the White House and me to the United Nations.

I have never planned my life. I have done my best to try to determine what God would have me do and do it to the best of my ability. I was settled comfortably now in the Congress of the United States representing Georgia's Fifth Congressional District. My civil rights experience gave me instant influence and respect. I was preparing myself to spend the rest of my working life in Congress. In mysterious ways that I could never anticipate all this was to change. I became like a leaf in a divine wind, blown hither and yon into a new career and given a new mission. Southern walls were coming down, but the cry for basic human rights, for peace, freedom, and justice from the oppressed of the world was beginning to be heard in the churches and synagogues of America.

The words of a British journalist and an African student, worlds apart and unknown to each other, were responsible for my being at the Georgia governor's mansion that beautiful spring day. That initial meeting led to my developing a working relationship with Jimmy Carter. I was there to apologize to Governor Carter for Jonathan Power's distortion of my comments about the New South in an article he had written; there he attempted to interpret the policies of Governors Carter, Askew, and Bumpers as promoting a new American version of British socialism. Power's writing had led Governor Carter to believe that I did not think very much of him, when it was only the notion that Jimmy Carter and the new southern leaders were socialist ideologues that I rejected. Powers had seriously misrepresented my views, and it was important for me to personally set the record straight.

When I visited Governor Carter to apologize for the misunderstanding, he took the occasion to ask my advice and opinion on United States policy on southern Africa. In a recent visit to California in his capacity as the Democratic Party Congressional Campaign chairman, an African student had asked his opinion on Namibia, Rhodesia, and South Africa. In the spring of 1974, few Americans had very strong feelings about Africa and few politicians would have been very knowledgeable on African affairs, so I was impressed that he had taken the question seriously enough to seek a serious answer.

I had come to know and admire Jimmy Carter as a

sincere and dedicated human being, but like many southerners and particularly black southerners, I had a feeling of
inferiority that could be both personal and geographic.
Georgia has led the nation in dealing with the problems of
race and continues to struggle aggressively with poverty.
Southern leaders have had to face issues on a daily basis
that most Americans have succeeded in ignoring.

Yet in spite of my respect for Jimmy Carter's intelligence, his disciplined life, and his religious convictions, it
was difficult for me to think of him as a possible president
of the United States. Neither could I think of myself as
actually formulating policy for our nation. But since it
looked like there was going to be a contest between two
Southern sons, Carter and George Wallace, I took the
opportunity to share with Governor Carter some of the
recent articles from *Christianity and Crisis* and the denominational statements of Protestant churches, all of which
based their human rights policies on words from the *Declaration of Independence,* that "all men are endowed by their
Creator with certain unalienable rights."

Our friendship grew slowly. I occasionally was asked to
assist with human relations problems in the state. On the
day Jimmy Carter chose to announce his candidacy for the
presidency of the United States, I was previously committed to address an honors banquet for the Lovett School in
downtown Atlanta. This was just across the street from the
Hyatt Regency where the Carter announcement was to
be made. I had planned to drop by for the announcement
and offer my congratulations on my way home. But just as
I was moving in to be seated for the Lovett School banquet, Jody Powell came over and asked if I would introduce Governor Carter for his announcement address. I
agreed to do so, and Jody asked if I could address the
Lovett students and parents before dinner rather than after,

so that Governor Carter's announcement could make the evening news.

Of course when introducing someone running for the presidency, you have to make a case for their being the next president of the United States. Even as I delivered my remarks to Lovett students, I was thinking up an argument for this seemingly impossible dream.

The next morning the headline of the *Atlanta Constitution* read, "Jimmy Is Running for What?" I found myself constantly explaining to my colleagues in Congress why I was supporting a southern governor. Not only did I find myself justifying my position on Governor Carter's candidacy to my colleagues, but I began receiving invitations from Iowa, Wisconsin, Pennsylvania, and Massachusetts to visit my colleagues in the House of Representatives in their home districts to explain why I supported Jimmy Carter for president.

It was as though politicians who had met Carter liked him and really wanted to support him, but they considered it risky because he was a southerner. My going with them to their constituents as a "son of the civil rights movement" offered them some security. Many acted as though they were afraid that something might fall out of the closet of any white southerner and jeopardize their own reelection. Even as I tried to maintain some distance and independence from the actual structure of the Carter campaign, I found myself visiting forty-one states with my congressional colleagues. During these visits I campaigned for their reelection and responded to questions by the local press that inevitably centered on the possibility of a Carter presidency.

American politics are supposed to be separated from religion, but this is a largely institutional separation. The average voter in this nation is strongly influenced by ideals and values which come from his or her faith and religious upbringing. In the early primaries, before there is major media coverage, the candidates visit small towns in an attempt to get votes and also establish contact with America's heartland, a land of people of faith with strong convictions about the future of our country. Voters' own religious convictions have a strong influence on their choice of candidates.

In part, because of this religious factor, Jimmy Carter began to do well, especially in New Hampshire and Iowa —states with early primaries. As a result of his living with families on the campaign trail, he began to hear clearly the concerns of ordinary people. He found his own sensitivity to the concerns and the rights of all people echoing through the kitchens and living rooms of a middle America—an America reeling with disillusionment over Vietnam, Watergate, and U.S. complicity with military dictatorships in Latin America. The idea of a government as decent and honest as the American people became both a hope for the future and a powerful expression of the latent American idealism which fired the campaign of Jimmy Carter.

Gradually I was becoming convinced that not only was Jimmy Carter a good man but that we actually needed him as president. Carter became more than the "favorite son of the South, stop Wallace" candidate that might end up as vice president on the Democratic ticket. From that time on, I found myself seeking opportunities to advance his candidacy.

Often we are blinded to God's will and guidance by our own prejudice. I was. Jimmy Carter spoke with a south Georgia accent, and he once shared with me that he was a friend of the sheriff of Sumpter County, Georgia. This sheriff was a man I remembered Martin calling the "meanest man in the world" because he turned on the fans in the jail on a chilly night when Martin asked for heat and blankets for young demonstrators arrested in the heat of the day, now shivering in the cool of the evening.

There were so many reasons for me, with my background and experience, not to trust or believe what Carter was saying. Only the Lord could have led me into the situations which led to my enthusiastic support.

I don't mean to imply that God is a partisan of the Democratic Party. I found myself in a similar situation in Congress when I supported Gerald Ford of Michigan as the House of Representatives designee for vice president upon the forced resignation of Vice President Spiro Agnew.

Ford was a conservative Republican with an anti-civil rights voting record, but for several weeks I found myself with him in the Congressional Health Clinic. He had hurt his knee in a skiing accident in Vail during the congressional recess, and I was suffering a pinched nerve from a long flight to Japan for an interparliamentary conference. As I spoke with him each day, I began to appreciate him as the kind of calm, stable leader that could help our country through the Watergate crisis that was just heating up.

Our accidents and regular meetings may have been coincidences, but I'm convinced that God uses such coincidences to bring people together for divine purposes. At that time, Gerald Ford seemed to me to be God's best for the country, in spite of his shortcomings. The same was true of Carter.

God uses all of us in spite of our weaknesses and imperfections, and no one need be perfect to be a part of God's plan. Politics has to be an arena for God's action. That action occurs through men, women, and events. I have tried to see the potential for good in every political event or person. No matter how tainted and compromised the party or government, the potential for some good remains. Any leadership can make life better for some of God's children.

Once Jimmy Carter became a front-runner in the campaign, his critics became more vehement. The ABC Movement (Anybody But Carter) began to stir among the more liberal elements of the Democratic Party. These were the very people who had been our strong supporters in the civil rights movement and who had backed my candidacy for Congress a few years earlier, and I found myself constantly answering critics. But by now, I was gaining confidence in my allegiance to Carter. I am never completely certain that I am right. Conviction grows through constant testing, and I am always ready to admit that I have made a mistake. But a meeting between the Congressional Black Caucus and Carter made clear to me something that I had felt instinctively but just couldn't put my finger on prior to this encounter.

Jimmy Carter had been invited to meet with the Caucus in a small chamber just off the floor of the House of Representatives. Each of the other Democratic candidates for President had been invited to a similar meeting. Most of these candidates were our colleagues from the Senate and the House of Representatives, but much to my surprise, each seemed to be unusually uneasy when alone in the room with twenty blacks, even black members of Congress whom they had known personally for years. There was nothing said specifically. In fact, they all agreed totally with the positions of the Congressional Black Caucus. On one standard question, "How many blacks do you have on your staff?" each of the liberal candidates answered, "One," except for the most liberal candidate, who was "looking for one."

When it came to Jimmy Carter, the group was somewhat hostile in the beginning. There was a reluctance to believe that a southern governor, especially a governor from Georgia, could ever win the support of the Congressional Black Caucus. Carter had been reluctant to toe the line on a number of liberal issues. He was reluctant to accept quotas to establish racial balance. He had reservations about the Humphrey-Hawkins Jobs Bill, which made the government responsible for full employment, and he talked about balanced budgets, which most of the Caucus viewed as a Republican code for avoiding domestic spending, particularly spending on poor people.

When Carter was finally asked the perfunctory "How many blacks on your staff?" question, he looked a little bewildered. He had not really counted, but a staff member answered, "Twenty-seven." Black staffers were members of the steering committee, the issues task force, and the fundraising, community organizing, press, and advance teams. The contrast was too great to miss.

Campaigns are challenging. They are about finding ways to determine leadership without bloodshed. They are never polite and seldom even civil. The 1976 presidential campaign was no exception. The Pennsylvania primary was the last possible opportunity to stop Carter within the Democratic party. Northern, liberal, and labor forces were strong in Pennsylvania, and former Vice President Hubert Humphrey was being championed as the alternative. But I was fully committed to holding Carter's coalition together.

I had many good friends in Philadelphia, among them the Rev. William Herbert Gray III. The Rev. Gray's father and grandfather had been close friends of the King family and were also prominent Baptist preachers at Philadelphia's Bright Hope Baptist Church. I also counted on Henry Nicholas, vice president of Hospital Workers' Union 1199, with whom I had helped to organize and settle a strike of hospital workers in Charleston, South Carolina in 1969.

I called Bill and Henry and asked them if they could gather a few mutual friends, friendly clergy, and labor leaders for me so that I could discuss with them the coming Pennsylvania primary and the attempts to stop Carter. We agreed on a date, and I went to Philadelphia thinking that we would be lucky to get twenty-five or thirty ministers and labor leaders together on such short notice, especially since our agenda ran counter to conventional wisdom and traditional leadership.

When I arrived at Bright Hope Church there were more than four hundred ministers and almost fifty of the more progressive union leaders who were tired of following the dictates of national organizations. They welcomed a direct appeal to their own leadership and intelligence. We left Philadelphia with a mobilization of ministers who were prepared to support Carter and take the message across the state. Carter won Pennsylvania, won the Democratic nomination, and in November won the presidency.

Shortly after the election, I joined a Congressional delegation to Africa for a conference of the African American Institute in Masero, Lesotho, a tiny mountain kingdom landlocked within the confines of South Africa and protected by the heritage of former British colonial rule. Here several hundred African and American leaders gathered to assess relations between Africa and America and project their hopes for the future.

While I was in Lesotho, much to my surprise, I received a phone call from WSB radio in Atlanta and was asked to comment live on the Morning Show about rumors that I would be offered an appointment as U.S. Ambassador to the United Nations. I honestly assured them that I had heard no such rumors and said that I was not interested. I had plans only to return to Congress to serve the Fifth Congressional District which had recently reelected me to a third term by a very generous margin.

That was also true, but my interest in the possibility of an ambassadorship was sparked.

The U.N. ambassadorship was not seen as a secure position. In the Congress I was secure and independent. I was also convinced that the big weakness in the Carter camp was that there was no one with any "inside" Washington experience. As a third-term member of the Congress I had learned quite a bit about Washington, the Congress, the press, and the Washington social set that manages to maintain a surprising influence regardless of which party is in power. I was sure I should remain in Congress.

On my return to Atlanta, I was asked to drop by the governor's mansion to brief Carter on my trip to Africa. When I finished my report on the hopes and expectations of the African leaders, he responded by saying, "That's why I'd like you to join my administration as a member of my cabinet and ambassador to the United Nations."

Believe it or not, I was still surprised. I tried to decline in favor of Congresswoman Barbara Jordan, who had so distinguished herself during the Judicial Committee hearings on Watergate. But Carter was very specific about what he wanted in a U.N. ambassador; in spite of my protestations and arguments about his needs in the Congress and my willingness to join his administration in the second half of his current term or in his second term, he insisted, "We may have only a few months to get the country moving in the right direction. There may not even be a second term. Whatever we are going to do must begin immediately. Frankly, I need you because of your relationship to Martin Luther King, Jr. and the civil rights movement. You can give our efforts on human rights an immediate credibility."

Jimmy Carter is a determined man, and it is hard to refuse him or refute such conviction. This, however, was no longer just Jimmy Carter, a man whom I had come to truly admire and respect during the campaign. This was now the President of the United States asking me to serve my country in a specific way. I saw the potential for basic human rights to become a major emphasis of United States foreign policy. This was for me a direct connection to the scripture which Jesus quoted from Isaiah as he began his ministry.

> The Spirit of the LORD is upon Me,
> Because He has anointed Me
> To preach the gospel to the poor;
> He has sent Me to heal the brokenhearted,
> To proclaim liberty to the captives
> And recovery of sight to the blind,
> To set at liberty those who are oppressed;
> To proclaim the acceptable year of the LORD.
>
> (Luke 4:18–19)

The most powerful government in the world taking human rights seriously had the potential of changing the world, the potential to bring peace on earth and goodwill to all people.

I could not easily say no, but neither could I say immediately yes. Jean had never moved to Washington, D.C. and had remained dedicated to her career in education. She would now have to give up her career and move to New York. I didn't know where we would live or where my sixteen-year-old daughter, Paula, would go to school. And what about my son, Bo, who was only four; what would it be like for him growing up in New York? These were questions I could not answer alone.

Carter volunteered to talk with Jean and discuss the situation with her. Of course, the same pressures of patriotism and faith were there for her as well. She could not say no. She was well aware of the reluctant journey which had led us to this point. She too was convinced that we were caught up in something much bigger than ourselves. And though we did not know what the future might hold, we trusted the God who held the future even as he had led us in the past.

And so, with plenty of hesitation and trepidation, but confident that once again we were being called by God to serve, we answered, "Yes." We were going back to New York.

My years serving as the U.S. Ambassador proved to be an affirmation of many things I believed in. Once President Carter determined that human rights would be an important cornerstone of U.S. foreign policy, the world began to change, and I found myself in the center of a hurricane of debate. It took awhile for the press and the nation to realize that Jimmy Carter was serious. Whether in South Africa, Central America, or the Soviet Union, our nation now would be concerned about how leaders respected and protected the basic human rights of their citizens.

An informed citizenry is an absolute essential for a democratic society. In order for people to change their minds and grow to understand the demands of a changing world, discussion is necessary. Discussion means controversy, and I often found myself at the center of controversy because I insisted on trying to explain a worldview which was shifting from a defensive cold war posture to an aggressive offensive for the rights of all people on the planet.

I knew we were on the right track, but I was reassured when the U.N. Ambassador from an especially repressive government said to me, "I must protest your position on behalf of my government. But I know that you are right, and though my government will criticize your government, my people cheer you and President Carter for standing up for what we all know is right."

Little did any of us imagine that we would see such dramatic changes in the world without the U.S. having to resort to violence. In Panama, the Middle East, southern Africa, and the Soviet Union a process was begun which would spread the light of freedom in many of the world's dark corners.

Gandhi's favorite hymn, "Lead Kindly Light," had been one of my favorites. Its words supported us in our decisions.

> *Lead kindly light, amid the encircling gloom,*
> *Lead thou me on!*
> *The night is dark, and I am far from home;*
> *Lead thou me on!*
> *Keep thou my feet; I do not ask to see*
> *The distant scene; one step enough for me.*

11

Blessed Are the Peacemakers

In the civil rights movement, I was always considered the conservative. In the Congress, I was viewed as moderate, because I refused to vote a strict party line with the Congressional Black Caucus and the liberal democrats who were my best friends.

Now I found myself in New York being branded by the so-called liberal New York media as a radical—even a fanatic—because I emerged as the Carter Administration's most visible proponent of human rights. It was a new role for me, and I was not at all comfortable with it. I felt that I was trapped by my understanding of the truth.

I viewed the world from the perspective of my friendship with students from all over the world at Hartford Seminary and from my associations in the World Council of Churches. The world was not an alien environment against which we had to defend ourselves as much as it was a place that was attempting to solve many of the same problems of human survival and development. We had been aspiring toward mutual goals with a great deal of success. I saw our role in the U. S. as providing vision and leadership.

Jean and I had considered going to Angola, West Africa as missionaries when we left seminary. I had followed events in Angola since my Sunday school days in New Orleans when our Sunday school helped to sponsor a school and mission station which was run by Rev. Henry McDowell, a black American pastor who had spent his entire life in Angola. Rev. McDowell retired at age seventy-five and had hoped that Jean and I could continue his ministry, but we ended up in Georgia. My interest in Angola led me to sponsor legislation in the House of Representatives to prohibit the sale of U.S. aircraft to Portugal since they were being used to kill the innocent people of Angola—people who only wanted the freedom to determine their own destiny.

Angola, unfortunately, became one of the most tragic victims of the cold war, and it appeared that the divisions of the church contributed to the confusion. In Angola, the Baptist Holden Roberto was working for the CIA. The Methodist Dr. Augustino Neto was being supported by the Russians. And the Congregational minister's son, Jonas Savimbi, was supplied with weapons by South Africa. It was a comedy of misunderstanding except that people were being killed by the thousands.

As I moved to New York, the South African and CIA factions were attempting to destroy the Gulf oil installations in the Cabinda Province of Angola, and the Cubans were defending Gulf Oil. This was in 1977 shortly after the OPEC oil crisis, and most of the U.S. oil supply was being generated in West Africa.

In my first national TV interview in New York, Dan Rather of CBS asked me, "What do you think of the

Cubans in Angola?" I answered casually, "Right now they seem to be a stabilizing force."

This was a reasonable view held by most of the U.N. community that knew anything about Africa. The killing had stopped and the oil was flowing. But this was counter to cold war ideology, and, therefore, I had my first scandal. It was not to be the last.

I was speaking of the world from a completely different point of view. Some said it was a "third world" point of view, but I was simply sharing the view of most of my friends and classmates who were serving in Christian missions around the world. They spoke the languages of the people to whom they ministered, and they had lived with the people now for most of the twenty years since we studied together at Hartford Seminary. I was always suspicious of most of the intelligence reports which I received because the data came from people whom we employed, and they will always tend to tell you what they think you want to hear. But my unorthodoxy continued to make headlines, and this was the last thing I wanted or needed.

I finally decided that if we were going to change the perspective of the nation from a "cold war" approach to the world to a human rights approach, then the discussion surrounding my controversies was probably good for the country. It certainly gave me a level of credibility seldom enjoyed by our United Nations ambassadors.

During the thirty-three months in which I served as U.N. ambassador, we were able to pass every single resolution we put before the Security Council. There was never a Soviet or Chinese veto, in spite of the fact that I was required to cast a U.S. veto on several occasions. The U.S. had not successfully introduced and passed a resolution before the U.N. Security Council since the Korean War.

Now the United States successfully introduced efforts

to begin a peace process in southern Africa which led to an independent Zimbabwe and Namibia. This was a direct outgrowth of our churches' missionary activity. All of the leadership of the liberation movement in Zimbabwe was trained in missionary schools by British and American missionaries.

Over six thousand black Rhodesians (now Zimbabweans) had received graduate training in British and American universities, but in their return home, they were not allowed to vote and were severely limited in their vocational and social possibilities. When they began to protest their treatment, they were jailed. When they organized to defend each other, they were called communists, and that made them subject to all sorts of violence and oppression. Many of them had read Marx and studied socialism in school, but I was convinced that they could be reached best through the Christian values of their early missionary teaching. After all, many of the same accusations were made against Martin Luther King in the early days of the civil rights movement. Any advocate for change and justice was thought to be influenced by communism.

But the Bible reads differently to those who are oppressed. We believe that "justice will roll down like waters and righteousness like a mighty stream." We read the story of God's deliverance of the children of Israel, and we are convinced that it can and will happen today, God willing. No one, however, had drafted a biblical theology of change, although in Latin America "liberation theology" was beginning to be formulated. Most advocates for change were trapped in the revolutionary language of communism. In reality, when offered an opportunity for democratic change through free and fair elections, most liberation movements demonstrated their true intentions toward reform rather than revolutions and chose elections.

It is a beautiful sight to visit Zimbabwe and Namibia

now to see black and white citizens struggling side by side to deal with the problems of development. Remarkably, there has been a capacity to forgive the sins of the past and move on to create a future together. Even now, after the harsh oppression of South African racism and his own imprisonment for twenty-seven years, Nelson Mandela is able to say, "There can be no revenge, reprisal, or retribution; we must move on together to build a non-racist South Africa."

Even in 1977 in my first visits to South Africa, I was well received, though I had publicly declared that I thought the government of South Africa was an illegitimate government since only 15 percent of the population had the right to vote, own property, or receive an education. The comments were criticized but never refuted. It was thought to be undiplomatic to speak the truth.

But speaking the truth in love is the only way to approach the problems of injustice nonviolently. And when the truth is spoken without judgement, but rather to point to the possibility of a "more excellent way" of living together as brothers and sisters in spite of the differences of race, class, or creed, there is the possibility of anyone accepting the potential of a new start. This is the way God deals with us as his children, and it is also the way that we must learn to deal with each other.

Africans have been able to adopt this philosophy far more successfully than the Middle East or Europe, but in America's response to victory in World War II, there is the same capacity to forgive and to move on together to rebuild a peaceful world, as we did through the Marshall Plan. This multi-billion dollar aid program paved the way for twenty-five years of successful growth and development for the entire world during the 1950s and 1960s.

Some would imply that there is something unique in this capacity to forgive, as though the Creator made distinctions in the redemptive capabilities of certain groups. But the harsh violence and hatred we see emerging in our own cities and in the conflicts of Liberia, Sudan, and Somalia or in Uganda under Idi Amin show us clearly that Africans are no better than anyone else. I think we clearly see the influence of the century of ministry and teaching by Christian missionaries who by their own love and sacrifice helped to demonstrate a new potential in the human spirit.

At the United Nations, I was very conscious of the potential to build new relationships between nations and peoples who perceived themselves as enemies. My experience in the church and in the civil rights movement convinced me that it was worth the effort to attempt to find some common ground with every potential adversary.

Jean and I played tennis regularly with the Soviet Ambassador and his wife. Ambassador Troyanovsky had attended Swarthmore College in Pennsylvania and played in his college tennis team. He and his wife, Tanya, met on a tennis court in Moscow and were avid competitors on the court. We played what we called "diplomatic doubles" where he and Jean teamed against Tanya and me, and we always split sets. When other colleagues at the U.N. discovered the outcome, they would playfully chide us, "Are the Americans afraid to beat the Russians, or are the Russians afraid to beat the Americans?" To which Oleg and I would reply, "No, we're both afraid of our wives."

The regular, friendly game of tennis meant that when there was a potential disagreement over U.N. resolutions or policy, we could usually discuss it privately and work out a reasonable solution that protected the interests of both countries. My approach to just about every problem was to discuss it until you could find a common ground that would allow us to live and work together. Ultimately, this is what has to happen when nations and groups disagree. No matter how much death and destruction, when the killing stops, there will still be some people left on each side who will have to learn to live together. There are really no winners and losers in any conflict. One side may seem to prevail for a season, even for a century, as is the case in the former Yugoslavia. But if tensions are not reconciled, the hatreds will be passed down for generation after generation until they erupt again and again like an active, smoldering volcano.

Conversation, negotiation, even the friendly competition on the athletic field or in the marketplace all serve as avenues of reconciliation. They help to release some of the tension and insecurity which flow from our differences. These tensions are prevalent within families, as well as between groups and nations, and learning to reconcile differences is one of the essential ingredients of civilization. The anger and violence between the sexes and between generations can be as devastating as that produced by racial and ideological conflict. It is absolutely necessary to learn to diffuse and reconcile differences without violence if families, neighborhoods, nations, and institutions are going to survive.

It was this conviction that finally led to the end of my United Nations service.

In the month of August, 1978, I was scheduled for my normal rotation as President of the Security Council of the United Nations. Fifteen nations serve on the Security Council with the victorious Allies of World War II, the U.S., the U.S.S.R., England, France, and China serving as permanent members and exercising a right of veto. The other ten seats rotate among the remaining member nations with each continent receiving two members. The presidency rotates in alphabetical order with each nation occupying the chair for one month.

We had been quite successful during my two previous

presidencies. We began the Anglo-American Plan for the end of the civil war in Rhodesia, launched the effort by the five western nations which eventually led to the independence of Namibia, began the sanctions against South Africa with an arms embargo, placed a U.N. peace-keeping force in Lebanon, and supported the efforts of President Carter on the Camp David Accords and the Panama Canal Treaty.

Because President Carter and Secretary of State Cyrus Vance believed in the potential of the United Nations to build support for U.S. initiatives, I was able to be considerably more activist than my predecessors at the U.N. Previous ambassadors were usually on the defensive in regard to Vietnam, the Middle East, or African issues. Fortunately, Carter and Vance were committed to restoring America's leadership in the international forum, so they not only welcomed my assertive role at the United Nations, they encouraged it, often to the dismay of the bureaucracy in Washington. The nations of the world were excited about the leadership role the U.S. had assumed and began to save their "pet issues" until it was my turn in the Presidency of the Security Council.

Stoney Cooks had been my friend since my days as executive vice-president of the Southern Christian Leadership Conference where he was chief of staff. We had been through a lot together, including Martin's death, the Poor People's Campaign, and three elections to Congress. He organized the efforts to help my dreams and prayers become reality.

Stoney is married to Harry Belafonte's baby sister, Shirley, and Harry invited us over to his home for a private dinner with his friend of long standing, Shimon Peres, then leader of the opposition of the Israeli government. Just a few weeks earlier, I had had breakfast with Moshe Dayan, the Foreign Minister of Israel. Both talked constantly about the "Palestinian problem" and why it must be solved if Israel was ever to live at peace with her neighbors.

But we were already engaged in too many controversial issues at the U.N., and Stoney always insisted that the Middle East was Washington's problem. It was much too emotional an issue to address in New York, and I agreed. There were many good reasons why an issue so delicate should not be handled in a multi-lateral forum like the U.N. But the U.N. Committee on Palestinian Rights was the only forum available to Palestinians in the United States, and they were tired of being ignored.

Normally, the Committee would have made its report in June or July under the Security Council Presidency of the Soviet Union or the United Kingdom. Nothing ever happens in New York in August. The weather is hot, and most of the diplomatic community heads for the hills unless there is an international crisis. So I was quite surprised when the British Ambassador informed me that I had better get ready, the Committee had requested a delay of their report until August when I was to preside over the Security Council.

When I received the report of the Committee on Palestinian Rights, I was pleasantly surprised to find that this was not the usual condemn-Israel-and-blame-them-for-every-problem resolution. There seemed to be an attempt to reach out for some sort of political accommodation.

For the first time, the PLO was offering a U.N. Security Council Resolution that accepted all previous U.N. Resolutions on the region. This included the resolutions which created the State of Israel and thereby recognized the Jewish state.

I was told by the Kuwaiti Ambassador, Abdullah Bishara, the present chairman of the Arab group, that this Resolution had come from Chairman Arafat himself and represented a potential change in PLO strategy. The only problem was that it also called for a Palestinian state, and I was sure that I would be instructed to veto any resolution that called for a Palestinian state without a carefully negotiated understanding of the powers and borders of such a state.

The resolution could not have come at a more difficult time for the Carter Administration. The economy was dragging, interest rates and inflation were rising, and the president had to focus on the economy. Secretary Vance was in the midst of negotiating a Strategic Arms Limitation Treaty with the Soviet Union, so it seemed best to try to postpone any consideration of the Palestinian resolution. It also seemed to me that it was important we not do anything to discourage what seemed to be a reaching out by the PLO for a more political approach to their problems.

Whenever there was a resolution about to be discussed in the Security Council under my Presidency, I invited the leadership of the group involved to have lunch at our residence in the Waldorf Astoria Hotel. Negotiations always proceed better when there is a "breaking of bread."

On this occasion I invited the Arab group leadership— the ambassadors of Egypt, Syria, Lebanon, Jordan, and Kuwait—to lunch to seek their assistance in arranging a postponement of the Security Council meeting. I was joined by Stoney Cooks and Ambassador Dick Petrie, the deputy ambassador of the U.S. to the Security Council.

The meeting involved a complete discussion of the situation. The Arab ambassadors agreed that it would be best to postpone the discussion, but they could not agree to the postponement without the concurrence of the PLO. They had a meeting scheduled with the PLO representative, Zehdi Terzi, a Columbia University professor who served as the PLO U.N. representative, on the coming

Saturday, and they would attempt to arrange a postpone-ment. They also said that they thought it would be neces-sary for me to talk with him personally to assure him that I wasn't simply trying to avoid the issue and that I agreed to raise it at a more appropriate time. I knew that such a meeting could be controversial, but acting as the president of the Security Council, it was mandatory that I meet with all parties in any dispute before the Council.

As the lunch ended, I agreed to come by the Kuwaiti Ambassador's home late Saturday afternoon, following the meeting of Arab ambassadors, to learn the outcome of their discussions. If it was necessary, I would be willing to talk with Mr. Terzi. Once again, a chain of events began which would change my life and launch me in a new direction.

For me, it would have been irresponsible to avoid going forward with this process. I had not initiated it or sought it out. There was clear indication from my meeting with Peres and Dayan that the heart of the problem of Israel's security was the Palestinian question. And at the time of the Camp David Accords a few months earlier, the Arab group had been insistent that the Camp David process not stop with Egypt. The slogan often reiterated was "No war without Egypt, but no peace without the Palestinians and Syria." I felt that I was being used by the PLO to bring their situation to the fore, but the fact that I was getting some of the same signals from both sides encouraged me to move ahead in spite of the risks.

There is an acceptable risk for war that is considered one's patriotic duty. Few men and women are able to see the risk for peace as a more powerful patriotic responsibil-ity. One is encouraged from childhood to be willing to sacrifice one's life in battle for one's country, but our society has no similar imperative to risk one's career and reputation in the struggle for peace. And we can only have peace when the peacemakers of a society are encouraged to act as courageously as the warriors.

At the time of my ordination into the Christian ministry some twenty-five years earlier, Rev. Homer McEwen had included in his Charge to the Ministry to, "Preach with your bags packed, for if you're ever fortunate enough to be used by the Spirit to share the full power of the gospel, you will probably be run out of town."

I thought of this charge as I walked over to Ambassador Bishara's home late one Saturday afternoon with my six-year-old son, Bo. I did not want to involve anyone else. The State Department had been told of the possibility of the meeting, but I had not asked permission or instructions. In order to get an official clearance, I would have had to get seventeen different bureaucrats to agree; not only was there not time for such a process, I felt that there were obligations to the Security Council Presidency that required the pursuit of any peace initiative. So I decided it was best to act on my own in this situation.

The meeting itself was quite uneventful. Bo played on the floor with the toys of Ambassador Bishara's son while I attempted to convince Mr. Terzi that this was not the time to bring forth such a significant resolution when the United States was not prepared to consider it seriously because of so many other priorities, foreign and domestic. Such an important issue required the full discussion of the government. Terzi explained that this was very important to the PLO and that he would have to get Chairman Arafat to approve any postponement. He said he would try.

There are no secrets in the U.N. community, but most of the significant work goes on in private. I was hopeful that my procedural discussions with the Arab group and Mr. Terzi could remain private, but such was not the case.

My meeting became a public issue, and I was involved in yet another public controversy and also a test of character.

I had enjoyed my service at the U.N. I felt we had accomplished a great deal, but now it was time for me to resign. I could not allow myself to become an issue that would distract the nation from the real challenges and opportunities which lay before us. To fight for a job, even the job of United Nations ambassador, was not worth any distractions from the peace process in southern Africa and the limitation of missiles and warheads with the Soviet Union.

The other tension was the strain on relations between the black and Jewish communities which had worked so closely together in the civil rights movement. This was the kind of issue that had the potential for attracting organized protests from some factions of the Jewish community. But if that happened, there was also the likelihood of major support for me being organized from Harlem and Brooklyn by some of my African American friends. So I went to Washington with copies of my resignation in hand, prepared to return to our home in Atlanta and continue working toward a more peaceful world as a private citizen.

12

When All God's Chillun Get Together

The challenge of each and every day is to ask: What in the world is God doing? How is God moving today, this day, at this time, and in the place where I happen to be? How can my personal thoughts and actions relate to the activity of God?

One thing on which science and religion agree is that nothing stands still. The universe is in motion. Trillions of particles in constant motion form the very fiber of our beings. Neutrons and electrons, swirling constantly within the spaces of our lives, help to create both physical and sociohistorical forces which are constantly "mak[ing] all things new" (Rev. 21:5).

After leaving the U.N., Jean, Bo, and I returned to Atlanta, Paula Jean entered Duke University, Andrea, a recent graduate of Georgetown Law School, returned home to begin preparations for the Georgia Bar, and Lisa worked at winding up her final year of electrical engineering at Howard University. Our family hardly missed a step due to my resignation. The business, lecture, and writing opportunities poured in, and it looked like we would enjoy being together as a family after years of struggle in public service.

I had not been home long when I was invited to a citizens meeting on the future of Atlanta. I went simply as an interested citizen, but I felt that I had made my contribution to public life and now ought to be concerned with providing some financial security for my family's future.

Atlanta was becoming somewhat polarized racially. The city and the suburbs were at odds. The state and federal governments were seemingly turning their backs on urban problems, and Atlanta, like every other major city, was beginning to feel the effects of dis-investment. All that we had worked for in the civil rights movement seemed endangered as the Reagan election victory deprived us of even the little hope that was beginning to emerge under Carter's human rights efforts.

After a lengthy analysis of Atlanta's political and economic situation by Maynard Jackson who was prohibited by law from seeking a third term as mayor, Mrs. Susie Labord, president of the Public Housing Tenants Association, took the floor and turned to me saying in ungrammatical profundity, "Andy, when you came to Atlanta you wasn't nobody. We took you in and made you somebody. We sent you to Congress, you been Ambassador to the U.N., but now we need you to be mayor. If you ain't learned enough to help us, can't nobody help us, and Lord knows we sho need help right now."

Once again I found myself unable to say no. Atlanta was in no real danger in my view. Maynard had been an excellent mayor, but he had pushed so many changes—necessary changes—that there was the same backlash emerging locally that helped elect Reagan nationally. Perhaps I could repair some of the strained relations and keep the city moving forward. The missing link was communication. Communication between business and government. Communication between races, classes, neighborhoods, and suburbs. Communication between Atlanta and the investment centers of the world.

Whenever the present agenda seems to be slowing down, there is always the potential for something new emerging on the scene. That was the situation when I first began to think about Atlanta's future beyond my term as mayor.

People must learn to live together in spite of their differences. I believe that Atlanta has been one city that has accepted that dream and moved with some success to make it a reality. Could it be that Atlanta could play some special role in the plan of God?

As I was about to conclude my second term as mayor of the city of Atlanta, things had gone very well for seven years. When I took over the city from Maynard Jackson in 1982, I inherited a sound base of urban development. We had just completed a new midfield terminal at Hartsfield International Airport, the mass transit program which I had helped to start while a Congressman was moving steadily along, and in general, things were in good shape.

However, once Ronald Reagan was elected president of the United States, there immediately were cutbacks on all federal funding for the cities. With the disappearance of federal funds, it became necessary to reach out to private investors from all over the world in an effort to provide jobs and economic opportunity for our citizens.

It is easy to quote Jesus' mandate to feed the hungry, but seldom do we stop to think how. The easy answer is by sharing existing wealth through government action. But this is what the nation rebelled against in electing President Reagan. The feeling was that the government was doing too much for poor people, minorities, and women. There were too many changes too fast in society, and people began to feel threatened by the changes and by the people who seemed to be the main beneficiaries of those changes.

In truth, the changes were more a matter of scientific and technological progress and the globalization of the economy. For the first time in the lives of most adults, the United States was no longer the clearly dominant economy. Japan and Germany were genuine rivals in wealth and productivity, and the formation of the Organization of Petroleum Exporting Countries (OPEC) meant that the U.S. could no longer dictate singlehandedly the course of world events. Everyone conveniently forgot that the world that now threatened us was one that we had consciously created at a time when the U.S. had a clear vision of a future in which people all over the planet could enjoy freedom and prosperity in a global climate of peace and security.

There was one missing link in the equation, however: justice. It was almost naively assumed that justice would automatically flow from freedom and prosperity. The rapid expansion of the global information network, now formalized in CNN, was already in existence. People in the most impoverished parts of the planet were being made aware of the wealth and luxury enjoyed by some of God's children through advertising, movies, radio, and television.

I recall being in Bogota, Colombia in 1967 and seeing street children for the first time. During the day I would see them begging for food and money with little tin pails. But then at night I would pass by them as they were huddled in front of a Sears store window, watching grade-B television movies of a world where children sat around a bounteous dinner table and were able to share an abundance of food and love provided by their parents. Even at that time you could see clearly what anthropologist Barbara Ward has described as "the rising tide of expectations."

The southern civil rights movement had captured the imagination of young and old around the world as we marched and sang "We Shall Overcome" and demonstrated that justice could prevail without violence. This was an essentially American vision, taught in our churches and schools, enforced in our courts and legislatures, and advocated in our editorials. Somehow we had never fully realized that these ideas and this vision of humanity would have to apply to everyone on the planet in order for it to be secure. For too many people in power, this vision applied primarily to men, and white men in particular. However, these were universal truths and people everywhere aspired to enjoy them.

Instead of continuing the vision and leadership of the postwar period through the 1960s, America, under first the Nixon administration and then the Reagan administration, sought to abandon any responsibility for global leadership. The Nixon administration abandoned The Bretton Woods Agreements of 1945. And the Reagan administration saw the whole of our national life as a military struggle against an "evil empire" and ignored the fact that our national security depended as much upon economic, cultural, and technical issues as on military ones. Money was taken from research, urban infrastructure repair, education, and housing to pour more and more into military expenditures in the name of defense and military security.

At the same time, even as most government policies proved disastrous and led to large financial deficits, homelessness, and the decline of U.S. competitiveness, huge surpluses of capital were being accumulated in the private sector. Other international economies based on exports thrived. Other countries with newly acquired oil wealth sought "safe havens" for their investment surplus in American real estate and industry.

As mayor of Atlanta I began an effort with the Chamber of Commerce, the Convention and Visitors Bureau, and the State Commission of Trade and Industry to attract new, private investment to the city of Atlanta. In my eight years as mayor, we attracted over seventy billion dollars in private investment, completed our expressway system, rebuilt Underground Atlanta, built and paid for a new city hall annex, continued the expansion of the mass transit system, and created more than five hundred thousand new jobs. For four years in a row we were voted the best city in America to start or expand a business. This was a city generating wealth, not just trying to redistribute existing wealth through taxation. The Atlanta experience confirmed Dr. Jane Jacobs's thesis in *Cities and the Wealth of Nations* that it is cities that create wealth, not national or state governments.

On the heels of this success, with every project completed on time and within budget and with 35 to 40 percent of all city expenditures going to minority and female owned businesses, I was looking at the possibility of running for governor of Georgia. Things were going very well, and Horace Sibley and Billy Payne, a former All American football player from the University of Georgia, impressed by the success of the city, wanted to come in to talk with me about hosting the Olympics in 1996. Both men were now successful Atlanta attorneys.

Most of my staff openly laughed at the idea. Our attitude was affected by the knowledge that the Montreal Olympics of 1976 supposedly had left the city with a seven hundred million dollar debt ten years later. But I had other images of the Olympics as well, and it was these Olympic visions that attracted me.

The Olympics in Berlin in 1936 are my earliest childhood memory. My father took me to the Orpheum Theater, where we climbed three or four flights of stairs to a segregated balcony. There I saw Jesse Owens, on Movietone News, win four gold medals in the 100-meter dash, the 200-meter dash, the broad jump, and the 400-meter relay. For my father and me, however, Owens' victory was not just over the other athletes in the events. Jesse Owens defeated Adolf Hitler's dreams of a German master race and the notions of white supremacy and racism in general.

Even for a four-year-old, these were not just abstractions. I had already been given a complete explanation of why I could not sit in the front of the bus or streetcar. There was also a German cultural center at the corner of Cleveland Avenue and Galvez Street, just one hundred yards from my home. Walking by at night you could hear them singing, *"Deutschland, Deutschland über alles . . ."* and shouting, *"Heil Hitler!"* from the street, so this was one of those life-defining events that remained with me for fifty years.

All these pent-up memories of Olympic dreams I had had as a child flooded through my mind as I was introduced to Horace Sibley and to Billy Payne. Billy's enthusiasm and idealism were apparent and contagious. He was Don Quixote in search of an impossible dream. As he described his intention of chasing this dream—with no expense to the taxpayers—and discussed the Los Angeles model of private-sector-sponsored Games, he won an immediate supporter. Once I had read Peter Ueberroth's book, *Made in America,* and saw clearly how a private sponsorship program could work, I was ready to go. I wasn't sure we could win the U.S. designation as host city from the United States Olympic Committee in 1996 with fourteen other cities in the running, but as I learned a few

things about Billy Payne, I became convinced that we
were right to try.

Billy is an intense competitor and hard worker. He
worries about every detail and strives for perfection in
everything he does. When still in his thirties, Billy had
already suffered a heart attack and undergone bypass surgery by the time I met him. In the wake of his recovery,
Billy took on the responsibility of raising funds for the
new sanctuary at his church. When this project was successfully completed, he said to his wife, Martha, "I just
hope I can do at least one more thing in life that is this
worthwhile." Then, relaxing at home after church one
Sunday, a mention of the Olympics came over the air and
Billy said to Martha, "We ought to try to bring the
Olympics to Atlanta."

It quite often takes a life-threatening experience to slow
us down long enough to appreciate the realm of the Spirit.
I began to see the hand of God transforming the suffering
of Billy Payne and his family into vessels of the Spirit.
When I suggested this to Billy, he quickly denied any
such lofty inclination, assuring me that he was not worthy
to be a part of such a vision. Yet everything he did suggested just that. This might be the kind of impossible
dream that could fit into what I felt to be God's plan for
Atlanta: I remembered always that "the Lord works in
mysterious ways his wonders to perform."

At Martha's urging, Billy talked to a broad cross-section
of his friends, including those who were most conservative and most practical and who on most issues would be
negative where any risk was involved. When most of this
group found the idea interesting and not at all insane, Billy
called his law partners and explained that he would not be
returning to work as previously planned but would begin
to work full-time, at the expense of his own savings and
with loans from friends, to make this impossible dream a

reality. Many other people were involved, and almost a dozen families sacrificed time and savings to develop the potential of this idea. It became an idea whose time had come.

Looking through the book of International Olympic Committee (IOC) members who would make the final site selection, I identified many of the seventy-three nations as countries where I had friends or had visited during my term as United Nations Ambassador. My influence could be helpful; however, it was the hard work and detailed planning by thousands of businesses, citizens, and young people that first captured the imagination of the visiting IOC Membership.

Those who carried the Olympic vision had the task of deciding just who we really were as citizens of Atlanta and what we had to say to the rest of the world. What was it that we truly stand for as a city, as a region, and as a people?

We soon realized that stadiums, hotels, airports, and transit systems, while clear assets, were not the stuff of which Olympic dreams are made. Indeed, for many of the IOC Membership, the Olympic vision passed down in modern times by Baron Pierre deCoubertin amounted to an almost religious quest for the peace and unity of all humankind through sports competition and cultural understanding.

Atlanta's global contribution is clearly in the area of human rights and the ability of people from many divergent backgrounds to live together in harmony. In today's world of ethnic violence and bloodshed, the message Atlanta could send to the multitude who will view some part of the Olympiad on television is the Olympic vision of all humankind living together in peace and prosperity with justice.

This is the message of Martin Luther King, Jr. that has

been heard around the world and which sprang from his Atlanta roots on Auburn Avenue and the Ebenezer Baptist Church. Martin's message is clearly in the tradition of the prophet Isaiah's exalted vision of the potential of people empowered of God.

Behold, I will create new heavens and a new earth.
The former things will not be remembered,
    nor will they come to mind.
But be glad and rejoice forever in what I will create,
    for I will create Jerusalem to be a delight
    and its people a joy.
I will rejoice over Jerusalem and take delight in my people;
    the sound of weeping and of crying
    will be heard in it no more.

Never again will there be in it
    an infant who lives but a few days,
    or an old man who does not live out his years;
    he who dies at a hundred
        will be thought a mere youth;
    he who fails to reach a hundred
        will be considered accursed.
They will build houses and dwell in them;
    they will plant vineyards and eat their fruit.
No longer will they build houses and others live in them,
    or plant and others eat.
For as the days of a tree, so will be the days of my people;
    my chosen ones will long enjoy
    the works of their hands.
They will not toil in vain
    or bear children doomed to misfortune;
    for they will be a people blessed by the LORD,
    they and their descendants with them.
Before they call I will answer;
    while they are still speaking I will hear.
The wolf and the lamb will feed together,
    and the lion will eat straw like the ox.

(Isa. 65:17–25 NIV)

In each and every time, God is revealing his will and unfolding his plan for his children. These plans have to become incarnate, they have to be made flesh. If so, why not in Atlanta? Why not now?

There is also the Atlanta of Margaret Mitchell's *Gone with the Wind* that has captured the imagination of peoples whose countries have been ravaged by war. The determination to rebuild life from the ashes of destruction is also a powerful message that the world has heard from Atlanta.

Approximately three-fourths of the population of the planet will view the Olympic Games in 1996 in Atlanta. These games mark the centennial of Olympic competition which were revived one hundred years ago in Athens, Greece. Now thanks to the expansion of television across the earth, almost four billion people are expected to view this spectacular event. We intend to share with them a vision of what can happen ". . . when all God's chillun' get together, what a time, what a time, what a time."

As we approach the twenty-first century, and as we face the continuing struggles against those principalities and powers which destroy families of nations and threaten the planet itself, there is certainly a divine potential in this enterprise. Not that Atlanta is a perfect model for the world or even for our nation: we have a long way to go. But the significance of Atlanta's success is that we have been able to come such a long way toward fulfilling our hopes, and we have not yet given up our dreams of *one nation under God, indivisible, with liberty and justice for all.*

13

A Way Out of No Way

Learning to live with God in the day-to-day struggle for existence is not the way most of us are brought up. Our parents and teachers do their best to make us self-sufficient, self-reliant, and very much in control of our own destinies. We are taught to admire the point of view of the poem "Invictus":

> Out of the night that covers me,
> Black as a pit from pole to pole.
> I thank whatever gods may be,
> for my unconquerable soul.
> In the fell clutch of circumstance,
> I have not winced or cried aloud.
> Under the bludgeonings of chance,
> my head is bloody but unbowed.
> It matters not how straight the gate,
> how charged with punishment the scroll,
> I am the master of my fate,
> I am the captain of my soul.
>
> (William Ernest Henley)

Looking back on some of the key events in my life, it all looks so easy. I assure you it did not seem easy at the time. Each of the major choices was accompanied by a great deal of anxiety and torment: seeking, searching, questioning, and worrying through sleepless nights and doubting days. I had struggled with my vocation, choice of a school, selecting a wife, and responding to a variety of callings from youth work to civil rights to Congress to the United Nations to mayor of Atlanta. I worried about the details and decisions that go with such choices.

Gradually I developed a depth of faith and religious insight that comes from knowing that God is present with me in life. I learned the importance of "the practice of the presence of God," to borrow the phrase of Brother Lawrence, whose devotional guide by that title describes his life in a monastery during the Middle Ages. But all of us are plagued by doubts and anxieties, by a sense of our own unworthiness.

It does seem awfully arrogant and presumptuous that any person should assume that the Maker of heaven and earth, the Lord God Almighty, has nothing better to do than to be concerned about lowly, trifling, lazy, and sinful me. And yet that is exactly what the gospel of Matthew claims: "Not one sparrow falls to the ground without your Father's consent . . . even the hairs of your head have all been counted" (Matt. 10:29–30 TEV).

Looking back over the years, patterns emerge and one learns, with difficulty, to discern the hand of God in one's daily existence. The will of God even becomes something we learn to look for and to pray for. But even the most religious and mystical of men and women write about "the dark night of the soul," those times when nothing makes sense and when the presence of God and the plan of God seem far removed.

I have been among the more fortunate. Life seems to

have its flow, and I am often able to be patient enough to go with that flow even when all about me is confused. I have such a certainty that "He's got the whole world in his hands" that I have learned to look for the dawning of a new day even in those darkest hours which precede it.

And this patience serves me where I am personally concerned and in my own personal life of faith. When it comes to my children, I am forced to my knees over and over again as I pray that they, too, will find that Inner Light to guide them on their way through life. It is for such strong-willed, strong-minded, independent souls that I seek to pass on the light of a life of faith.

The wisdom and experience of men and women seem to lead us in circles. Things change and priorities shift often with little overall improvement. The real breakthrough to new levels of faith, mercy, and justice are reached when the power of God enters the human situation. I have tried to illustrate this in the events of my own life, which could only have occurred with the guidance of God and a sensitivity to the shaping of this life to better reflect the purposes of the kingdom of God. Sharing some of the lessons of faith and life that have been so meaningful for me is my objective in this book.

When Andrea, my oldest daughter, was five years old we lived in New York and were faced with the dilemma of how to get her safely to school. I had just been reading Søren Kierkegaard's *Fear and Trembling* and his description of the testing of Abraham when God demands that Abraham offer his son Isaac as a sacrifice. This story might first seem like a very primitive approach to faith, except that the testing of Abraham required that nothing, not even his beloved son, should stand in the way of his obedience to God. It was only after Abraham proved his willingness to risk his son that he discovered the ram in the bush and received God's guidance that the ram be substituted in sacrifice.

Andrea was to attend Public School (P.S.) 154, which was four city blocks from our home and required crossing a major avenue. Did this situation present a modern parallel to Abraham's test of faith? I wondered. Did this story have anything to do with the tendency parents have to overprotect their children? I was not sure, but I had had Kierkegaard's book for over a year. Was it just a coincidence that I chose to read it at this time in my life, or could there possibly be some message in it for Jean and me with regard to our children?

With great fear and trepidation, I suggested that Jean walk Andrea to school for the first week and that we then trust her to God. By the third day, Andrea had organized a little rat pack of her five-year-old classmates to meet at the corner of our house to walk to school together. God had rewarded our faith by providing protection for our child even in New York City in 1960. That decision has guided us with the raising of all our children. Not only did Andrea successfully negotiate her way to P.S. 154, but later she and Lisa, our second daughter, were willing sacrificial lambs in the desegregation of Atlanta's private schools.

Years later, Paula, our youngest daughter, who felt she had been somewhat sheltered through life as the baby girl, insisted on volunteering with Habitat for Humanity to teach in Uganda after her graduation from Duke University. This really put us to the test. It was 1985; Uganda had just gotten rid of Idi Amin, but a rebel faction still was waging war against the government of Milton Obote. Of all the countries of Africa, Paula could not have picked one in a more precarious political situation.

I was somewhat consoled by the fact that up to that point, even in times of war and civil strife, the representatives of humanitarian groups like Habitat, UNICEF, the

Red Cross, and the many Christian missionary groups that served Africa had always enjoyed respect and protection. The thing that was so frightening about Uganda, however, was that there were roving bands of Amin's mercenaries loose across the land. No one knew where they were likely to show up.

But teaching was Paula's calling. I certainly had not suggested it. She was my baby girl, and yes, maybe she had been somewhat protected by Lisa and Andrea, but not nearly as much as she pretended. Paula went to Atlanta's public schools where she had encountered a broad cross-section of Atlanta's population. She had gone to the United Nations School in New York at age sixteen and been thrust into foreign policy debates where she was challenged to explain the Nixon, Ford, and Kissinger policies on Vietnam, South Africa, the Cuban Embargo, and our refusal to recognize Palestinians. Attending the United Nations school was a completely different life from cheerleading at Southwest High School in Atlanta with kids she'd grown up with.

I was so moved when Paula was commissioned as a missionary by First Congregational Church, United Church of Christ. I can be very emotional on occasions of religious significance; "my cup runneth over" very easily. I am always aware of the divine potential of any moment, but usually it was an awareness of the Lord doing something special with me and my own sense of inadequacy. But this was now my baby daughter. I could trust God in New York or Atlanta, and maybe with difficulty on the Ivory Coast, Tanzania, or Zimbabwe, but inside I was crying, "Why of all places must she go to Uganda?"

As a parent, the challenge of trusting my children to God's power and love is a far more ominous task than trusting God in my own life. But because my family has seen the Lord "move in mysterious ways his wonders to perform," it is important to share some of this story.

Paula went to Uganda, where she taught sixty children. There were no books, blackboard, or paper except the rolls of brown wrapping paper I would send whenever someone was traveling there. Also, Sabena Airlines occasionally ferried supplies to her without cost. Paula was in Uganda through two changes in government and considerable violence and suffering, yet she never had an experience which seriously threatened her. Not that she was not frightened or challenged by loneliness, by bats crashing into her window during a storm, and many other unusual experiences in the small Ugandan town of Gulu. Now when she sings "Amazing Grace" and gets to the verse, "Through many dangers, toils, and snares, I have already come, 'twas grace that brought me safe thus far, and grace will lead me home," she has her own wealth of personal experience of the awesome deliverance of God.

Back on the home front, we had no choice but to trust God or go crazy. We had no phone contact with Paula for almost a month. We knew there was a war going on and that one of the generals was from her area. Fortunately for us, so was the Ugandan Ambassador to the United Nations, Olara Otunu, who happened to be from Gulu and whose parents still lived there. God knew just how much we could bear, and whenever we seemed to be on the edge about to go overboard, Ambassador Otunu or someone from the Mennonite missionaries who had short wave radio contact with the area would call and give us word that Paula was all right.

I came to trust anew in the wise spiritual, "I know the Lord will make a way, oh yes he will. He'll make a way out of no way."

Jean and I have lived through Andrea going to school alone at five and going to Europe at fourteen and again at seventeen with a friend. She made it through Swarthmore College and Georgetown Law School. Then through the Team Defense and the NAACP Legal Defense Fund she took on death penalty cases in Georgia. She too spent a couple of years traveling around Africa, visiting schools and churches as Africa Secretary for the United Church of Christ Board of World Ministries before settling down with a family in Washington, D.C. I will always believe that Andrea's security and success began when we trusted her to God as she walked to P.S. 154 in New York at five years of age.

Standing in the parking lot at Purdue University in 1975, I held my daughter, Lisa, close as tears streamed down both our cheeks. Lisa was a soft, gentle homebody type who had chosen to study engineering in Indiana. It all seemed so incongruous. Whereas Andrea was outgoing and independent, Lisa always seemed more fragile, and I agonized over leaving her so far away from home. Yet when I think about it now, I realize that it was six-year-old Lisa who bravely integrated the segregated private schools in Atlanta.

The public schools were desegregated and the church-related schools were in danger of becoming a haven for the children of racists. The schools declared they had an open policy, but no black children had met their requirements.

We were persuaded to seek admission for one of our children. We chose Lisa who had just completed kindergarten at Spelman College's preschool program. We felt they couldn't possibly reject a child that young.

She passed all their school-designed tests but the principal recommended that she repeat kindergarten because she said Lisa didn't score quite as high as their children, and they wouldn't want the first black child to fail.

Confronting racism for yourself is one thing; subjecting

your small daughter to it required some real soul searching. Here again was the challenge to trust God to take care of our children. It was the Abraham-Isaac story all over again.

We made the decision to allow her to attend, but insisted that she be placed in the first grade since she had met all their so-called requirements. Lisa excelled academically along with her sister Andrea and several other black children who were then admitted. They encountered unpleasant experiences, but they also had very positive relationships with many children and teachers. I believe they acquired an inner strength that helped to prepare them for future challenges.

Lisa certainly met that challenge when she entered a non-traditional profession for women by choosing engineering, and then again when she was such a strong support for me during her mother's illness.

It does seem easy and almost idyllic looking back on our childrearing years; we have three wonderful daughters, married to outstanding young men of faith and character. We can easily forget the nights we stayed awake waiting for them to come in or the trips they took to Myrtle Beach, Jamaica, and other college vacation spots that contribute to parents' gray hairs and heart trouble. All that is long forgotten, and parenting would now seem like a piece of cake except that we still have one more child. The anguish and anxiety that should be all behind us is now magnified by the geometric progression of problems to which young black males fall victim.

Bo Young is my child. All of my strengths and weaknesses stare back at me each time I look at him. When he speaks, I hear my own rebellion and defiance of the *status quo,* my determination to be my own man. I sense some of my recklessness, and I pray that God will save him from himself, in spite of himself, as God saved me from myself, in spite of myself.

The irony of strong personalities is that God needs them. In a world where God is making all things new, the men and women who dare to serve God and do things in a different way from their fellows are often chosen for special blessings of service and opportunity. And until such strong wills are ready to submit to the will of God, parents and loved ones remain anxious and prayerful.

I should have known what to expect from such a child when Bo took charge of the Congress at two and a half years old. Jean was having a difficult time coping with his energy and spirited activity, so I would take him to Washington with me while Congress was in session. On one occasion when the usual confusion and loud talking was prevailing, Bo streaked down the aisle, went to the podium, and began to pound the Speaker's gavel. House Speaker Carl Albert took it with good humor and presented the gavel to Bo, congratulating him for restoring order.

Is the world more complex? Is it naive to believe, as I do, that all evil can be overcome? And what about the cross? Can redemption come to the world by unearned suffering? Yes, I know the anguish of Abraham as he struggled with his willingness to offer Isaac in sacrifice. I also know of the faith of Abraham, "that God can make a way out of no way," but the time of waiting on the Lord, the time of enduring the anguish of free choice remains difficult. As I read that story, I think of Isaac as a young adult not unlike my son. There is some scriptural evidence which points toward that conclusion. The previous chapter of Genesis takes Hagar's son up through marriage and family and then returns to the story of Isaac and Abraham. Isaac is encouraged to carry the wood for the burnt offering, hardly a task for a small child. Isaac must at least be a teenager at the time of the call to sacrifice.

There is a time in life when father-and-son conflict is inevitable. The growing young adult male must challenge the authority as well as the worldview of the father and the previous generation. Not to do this is to betray the process of God for the fulfillment of creation.

Parenting teenagers has always been a challenge, it seems. The lesson we must learn is that *to love is to listen.* There comes a time when you cannot decide for your children and you cannot determine their destiny. To try to do so is only to interfere with their search for God's purpose in their lives. You can only listen and pray. It's surprising how much of your better influence has prevailed. But you can only know this as you listen.

When Lisa was a baby, I was doing a lot of traveling, and I was greatly disturbed that when I came home, she would cry as I attempted to pick her up. During this time I read an interesting article on the need to respect children as persons. I remember that the writer challenged parents to listen to each child at least five minutes a day. Not talk to each child, but listen to each child. It is amazing how much they know and how many of the lessons of life they learn from your life and actions. Parenthood is not only being close to one's children; it is being willing to let go and trust them to the Lord.

I decided I had to find the time to listen to the needs of this child who withdrew from me because I kept leaving her. She was only three but I decided to take her traveling with me for a weekend. I combed her hair, cared for her, devoted concentrated time and attention to her. There was a transformation in our relationship after this experience.

It is amazing how much children understand and how many of the lessons of life they learn from your life and actions. Parenthood is not only being close to one's children; it is respecting them as individuals, responding to their special needs, and being willing to let go and trust them to the Lord.

As a young man I was determined to find out for myself just what values I wanted to incorporate into my life. For instance, my family was extremely religious. We went to church every time the church door opened. It was an absolute moral obligation against which I rebelled. I challenged Sunday school teachers with my doubts and questions as far back as I can remember. At Howard University, I only went to chapel on rare occasions, but it was also during this period of absence from the church that I engaged in some of my more serious searching about life's meaning.

When I finally began to understand the Christian faith and the relevance of Christ in my life, it led me to a level of commitment that even my very religious parents found difficult to accept. They wanted me to accept the same level of commitment to the Church that had been so meaningful in their lives, but they were not willing to see me move a step beyond conventional commitment to an understanding of holy obedience and total commitment which I had come to believe as my path to service and salvation.

So it is with most of us as parents. It is difficult for us to pray and really mean, "Not my will, but thy will be done," when it comes to the commitment of our children to the will of God, the plan of God, and the purpose of God in their lives.

I must confess, though, that in spite of my parents' anxieties about my career choices, I have always believed that it was my mother's prayers that led me "through many dangers, toils and snares." When I went away to college, it was quite a traumatic event for my mother. In addition to being only fifteen years old, I had hardly begun to take my studies seriously or develop the maturity required to be on my own. Her response to the situation was take it to the Lord in prayer. For the entire four years that I was in college, she began every day with a visit to the Catholic church on her way to work. Even though we are Protestants, she daily lit a candle and knelt to pray for my protection and guidance. Those prayers have indeed been answered far beyond my deserving. My mother's example and my own young adulthood experiences serve to help me as a father as I attempt to guide my children.

My children will pay no more attention to me or accept my opinions and ideas about the future than I was willing to pay to my parents. My hope for my children must be that they learn to respond to the still, small voice of God in their own hearts. I must trust that God will somehow direct, guide, and protect them as he did me and all the sons and daughters of Abraham, from Isaac throughout all generations.

God can still "make a way out of no way."

This affirmation has become real to us as a family in the past few years. Our trust in God has almost always had a social or political focus. Our personal faith was tested in the course of our efforts to engage in the social aspects of the gospel, and while this required a tremendous amount of personal prayer and soul searching, there was always the idea that what we were doing was a matter of our own choosing to interpret the will of God in a particular manner. Technically, we could have chosen another form of ministry or a different kind of challenge. But on July 26, 1991, all that changed. We were confronted with a deeply personal challenge from which there was no escape.

After three wonderful weeks together on a business trip to Zimbabwe followed by a weekend in the Bahamas with all our children, their spouses, and our grandchildren, Jean was awakened at home by severe stomach pains. Normally we would have attributed this to the strain of travel and the excesses of food and family in the heat of the Bahamas. But since we had been in Africa, there was the possibility of some strange virus or parasite disturbing her digestion, so I insisted on going to the emergency room at Crawford Long Hospital to get Jean checked out before I went to work.

Jean had never been ill. She had natural childbirth with each of four children and spent only a couple of days in the hospital with each. Serious illness was beyond our comprehension. You can imagine the shock when the doctor told me that there was a tumor blocking her intestine and that an emergency operation was necessary. He also added that in his years of experience such tumors were almost always malignant.

I was still hopeful as she went into surgery. We had been together almost forty years. Jean was really the backbone of our family. There was no way we could conceive of life without her vivacious, energetic spirit. But after the operation, the surgeon informed me that there was an indication that the malignancy had spread to her liver. He was very sensitive to our situation but suggested that chemotherapy might slow the spread of the cancer. He explained that the risk and success rate of chemotherapy and surgery were such that we should make the most of the time that we had left and make life as meaningful as possible for the next few months. Jean should have at least six months and possibly as much as a year to live with colon cancer that metastasized to the liver. I was numb.

Jean was still in intensive care as I received this message. I walked almost entranced by the horror of this announcement, and I passed the little chapel in the hospital. I entered and fell to my knees at the altar and finally let go of the tears that had welled up in me as a result of the most intense strain of my life. I had been somewhat prepared for Martin's death. He never let us forget what was at stake. I was even very philosophical about the possibility of my own death. I had been happy and surprised to turn fifty, but I could not live without Jean. Her leaving us was a tragedy that no one could consider.

As I ran out of tears and dried my eyes, I looked down at the open Bible on the altar and began to read Psalm 103.

> Bless the LORD, O my soul;
> And all that is within me, bless His holy name!
> Bless the LORD, O my soul,
> And forget not all His benefits:
> Who forgives all your iniquities,
> Who heals all your diseases.
>
> (vv. 1–3)

It was as though each word of this familiar psalm leaped off the page and into my heart. As is the case for most of us, we are lured by the hymns and anthems which emphasize, "Bless the LORD, O my soul," but until we are really confronted with a life-threatening illness, we don't pay much attention to the affirmation "He forgives all our sins, and He heals all our diseases." Now, my concern was the healing of Jean's cancer.

I remembered my experiences with Mrs. Hadley and her cancer years before in Beachton, Georgia. She was given a few months to live and lived at least thirty years longer and died in her late eighties. I wasn't sure what the prescription was, but one thing seemed clear: we must all be determined as a family to win this battle.

There was some evidence in heart attack victims that those who were well-loved had a much better recovery rate than those who had problem relationships or who were in need of love and affection. Also, we were too highly visible in Atlanta to keep secret such a serious crisis. Our friends responded immediately, and several churches across the community remembered us in their prayers. Even the newspapers respected our desire not to have any publicity, but the word spread nevertheless. We soon realized that we were surrounded by an extremely loving and supportive city. A family at prayer that is supported by a loving community is a powerful healing force, especially when backed up by good medicine and a network of nutritional and herbal approaches to the disease. Jean took charge of her own healing with the able assistance of some of the world's best oncologists and surgeons. But it was her life to live, and she didn't just sit back and do as she was told. She began to listen to her own body and use her own mind and the power of her spirit to direct her recovery.

A life-threatening illness forced us to a new level of religious sensitivity and awareness. Perhaps we and others should find ways to always be so sensitive to the spiritual realities, but nothing dominates one's attention like a doctor's death sentence. We've learned that once anyone begins to pay attention to the healing powers of faith and medicine, he or she is on the way to wholeness.

The church as a healing community comes to bear on an illness in an amazing way. As people heard of our situation we received wonderful letters and cards of encouragement, but also tracts and literature on health and healing, and finally two phone calls from dear friends from both coasts. Dr. John Maguire, chancellor of Claremont University in California, put us in touch with one of the best surgeons on the west Coast. Dr. Levi Watkins, associate dean of surgery at Johns Hopkins Medical Center, offered to pull a team of Johns Hopkins specialists together to offer an evaluation of Jean's medical condition. As a youth in Montgomery, Alabama, Levi had been a member of Dexter Avenue Baptist Church and had assisted Martin and the Montgomery Improvement Association by helping to clean the cars in the car pool.

We accepted the offer from Levi and Johns Hopkins because it was closer geographically and because Andrea and Paula were living in Washington, D.C., only forty miles from the hospital. The result of the evaluation offered the first real medical hope that we had received.

Dr. James Sitzmann of Johns Hopkins, who had specialized in liver surgery, thought that Jean's cancer was operable if it had not spread beyond the liver. He suggested six months of general chemotherapy to curtail the spread of the disease. If after six months there was no indication of the disease spreading, he thought he could operate and remove the tumors from her liver.

At times I thought that the chemotherapy was worse than the disease. I still think that there is something terribly primitive about the approach of chemotherapy, but for now I thank God for it and Dr. Douglas Collins who administered it. Jean also became a vegetarian, drank Chinese herb teas, and developed a pattern of prayer and meditation to support the work of the traditional medical wisdom. So much of our reading pointed to a positive attitude as a major contributor to healing that we did not neglect the spiritual aspects of her healing.

We truly believed she would be healed. But our faith did not depend on her wellness though we sought every way possible to restore her health. Jean discovered a new serenity in her faith that allowed her to understand the meaning of "Thy will be done." She frequently explained to her doctor that life with hope is a much better life, no matter how short, than one with despair.

The approach to her illness had to be an approach to the whole person: body, mind, and spirit. The mind and the spirit play such an important role in the growth, development, and healing of the body. We were determined to use every resource at our command, but especially the power of prayer.

Now two years later, Jean is once again running full speed ahead. She completed the operation which successfully removed five tumors from her liver. She is now free of medication and malignancy according to the past two six-month CAT scans.

The effort to come to grips with the evils of cancer and the experience of confronting social and political evils in society has all been enlightened by our sensitivity to the hand of God moving anonymously and mysteriously through our lives and our relationships. None of the success and survival that we have enjoyed over these past decades would have been possible without understanding and sensitivity to the power and presence of God in our daily existence.

We also shudder when we think of what might have happened had it not been for R. K. Sehgal and Law Engineering. The day I retired from the mayor's office, all our health insurance was cancelled. We had no retirement, no savings beyond our home, and a very expensively educated family.

I was introduced to R. K. by the Indian Ambassador to the U.N., Rikki Jaipal, who had been one of the people who helped me to understand the more subtle dynamics of U.N. politics. R. K. had come to the U.S. as a seventeen-year-old from India to study engineering at Auburn University.

It is another miracle that he not only survived Alabama in the sixties but went on to become chairman and CEO of the distinguished southern engineering firm in Atlanta founded by Thomas Law.

Under R. K.'s leadership, Law Companies became

truly international with the acquisition of Sir Alexandor Gibb and Partners, Ltd., a British-based firm with offices in forty countries.

I was retained as a consultant for the acquisition because many of the offices were in Africa and the Middle East where I had worked as Ambassador.

Moving from preaching to engineering is not such a great leap, since both require fresh water, electricity, roads, and buildings to "feed the hungry, clothe the naked, heal the sick," and set at liberty those who are oppressed. As a member of Congress I helped on many important environmental regulations. As ambassador I helped package financing for development of World Bank projects of water resources, a fertilizer plant in Nigeria, and a hydro-electric power installation for Argentina, all because I saw the inter-relatedness of religion, politics, and economics for the development of opportunities for God's children all over the earth.

As vice-chairman of an international engineering and environmental consulting firm, I continued to work toward the fulfillment of opportunities to improve living conditions globally.

But the employment and service opportunity became all the more important in Jean's illness because it provided health insurance which made the world's best medical care a possibility.

Health was always something we took for granted. We had no history of serious illness in the family. But an unemployed mayor at sixty years old can find it almost prohibitive to get individual insurance in today's market.

At each stage of life, God has provided for our needs in every challenging situation. Time after time, we have faced despair with no sense of direction, only to wait patiently on the Lord to make a way where there is no way.

At this point we are not sure what the future may hold

for us, but we know very well the God of Abraham, Isaac, Jacob, and the prophets. We know the God of love and mercy who is revealed in Jesus Christ. It is our experience and testimony that he lives and that the Spirit of God continues to be active in the events of God's children, whether those events are social, political, economic, or personal. Whether events involve governments, academic institutions, corporations, hospitals, churches, or the principalities and powers of our time, God is still able to make a way out of no way.

I have tried to give the reader some of the clues that I have learned as to the activity of God and the plan of God in our world. God is not through with us yet. We may not know what the future holds, but we know who holds the future, and we are expecting to be a part of that future, however God wills to use us.

Notes

Introduction

1. Thomas Kelly, *Testament of Devotion* (New York: Harper & Bros., 1941), 29.
2. St. Augustine, *Confessions,* trans. R. S. Pine-Coffin (London: Penguin Books, 1961), 38.

Chapter 2: On Kings Mountain

1. Kahlil Gibran, *The Prophet* (New York: Alfred A. Knopf, 1923, renewed 1951), 17–18.

Chapter 3: Answering the Call

1. Ralph Abernathy, conversations with author. This quote, like most of the other material from movement participants quoted in this book, is from my personal recollections of conversations, meetings, discussions, workshops, training sessions, speeches, sermons, and the like. Many of the ideas that formed the foundation of our movement were rehearsed in countless strategy sessions, and delivered over and over again in countless speeches and sermons throughout the course of the movement. Many of these same ideas later found their way into print in books by Martin and other movement figures. Here, however, I am, unless otherwise noted, quoting from my memory of what participants said, rather than what might later have been written in a book. All such occurrences will be noted as "conversations with author."

Chapter 4: Not My Will

1. Martin Luther King, Jr., conversations with author.

Chapter 5: Changing the World

1. James Bevel, conversations with author.

Chapter 6: Breaking Down Walls

1. Martin Luther King, Jr., conversations with author.

Chapter 7: Building Leaders

1. Frederick Douglass, *Narrative of the Life of Frederick Douglass: An American Slave, Written by Himself* (New York: Mentor Books, 1968), 79.

Chapter 8: Bless Those That Persecute You

1. Richard Attenborough, Selected, *The Words of Gandhi* (New York: Newmarket Press, 1982), 121.
2. Martin Luther King, Jr., conversations with author.